TURN
CLICKS
INTO
CUSTOMERS

TURN CLICKS INTO CUSTOMERS

Proven Marketing Techniques for
Converting Online Traffic into Revenue

Duane Forrester

New York   Chicago   San Francisco   Lisbon   London   Madrid   Mexico City
Milan   New Delhi   San Juan   Seoul   Singapore   Sydney   Toronto

ISBN 978-0-07-163516-5
MHID 0-07-163516-5

McGraw-Hill books are available at special quantity discounts to use as premiums and sales promotions, or for use in corporate training programs. To contact a representative please, e-mail us at bulksales@mcgraw-hill.com.

This book is printed on acid-free paper.

Turn Clicks into Customers by Duane Forrester is not sponsored, endorsed, or approved by Microsoft.

C o n t e n t s

Foreword

Traffic Is Not Your Problem!

FOR OVER A DECADE I have helped hundreds of companies come to the realization that they don't have a traffic problem. Bringing visitors to your Web site (or store) is a means to an end. Your goal is not to increase the number of people who visit your Web site but to get more sales, more leads, more subscribers; anything that produces more revenue.

I recently met with an organization that had 60,000 visitors a month to its Web site. Just about 90 percent of those visitors looked at more than one page—a good sign that they thought the site was relevant to their needs. That left 54,000 potential visitors to convert. At the time, the organization converted only about a 1,000 of these clicks into customers. Clearly, not everyone who visits your Web site is there to buy. Some are seeking customer service and some are doing digital window shopping, but a good 30 to 70 percent are there not because they have time to waste, but because they have some interest in your product or service. That leaves an opportunity to focus on converting into customers some of those 20,000 plus who are in the market to buy. If all you did was work on converting 500 of those, you'd increase your business 50 percent. That, my friend, is very doable!

The very first company my business helped to increase conversions was a magazine subscription reseller that took its site from a 1.11 percent conversion rate to a 4.93 percent conversion rate. The reseller is still in business today, while its competitor from the mid- to late 1990s and which raised $100 million or so, is out of business. Here's an example from the other end of the spectrum: Overstock.com came to me and my partners to help it convert more clicks into customers. We found one hole on Overstock's Web site that caused over 91 percent of people to leave from a particular page. The solution was changing one single graphic on the offending page. That one change made Overstock.com over $25 million. Yes, over $25 million!

You have this opportunity to turn your traffic, all those clicks, into customers. Duane Forrester's *Turn Clicks into Customers* will show you how. Most businesses will find it is much easier to double their conversion rates than to double their traffic. Can you afford not to be one of them?

Bryan Eisenberg

Writer for the *New York Times* and *Wall Street Journal*
and the bestselling author of *Call to Action,*
Waiting for Your Cat to Bark? and *Always Be Testing*

Acknowledgments

I'D LIKE TO RECOGNIZE some folks in this section—my award speech, if you will. I'll try to keep it short, but these people do deserve the shout-out.

No book is a creation of one individual, though one name may appear on the cover. On my journey to the completion of this book, which began over a decade ago, many people have influenced me.

First and foremost I credit my success to Bill Hartzer. When I asked him if I should use the content that eventually became my first book (*How to Make Money with Your Blog*) to publish an e-book, his straightforward, Texan answer was, "Anybody can produce an e-book; get a publishing deal and you're an expert." I am glad I followed his advice.

To the entire past and present crowd at www.searchengineforums.com, thanks. I have learned much, and I continue to learn from you. The entire board of directors at SEMPO (Search Engine Marketing Professional Organization) deserves thanks for helping me view our world from a higher elevation. I remain humbled by your knowledge and willingness to share.

Thanks also to Shawn Wells (for my first "paid for" gig as an online marketing manager) and Mike Sandalis, for encouraging me to learn search marketing, thereby exposing me to all forms of online marketing, and reminding me that while learning is fun, making money by applying the knowledge is even more fun!

I also want to express thanks to Jeremy Schoemaker, Khalid Saleh, Ben Jesson, Karl Blanks, Rand Fishkin, Rae Hoffman, and Stephan Spencer, not only for agreeing to be interviewed for this book, but also for sharing freely of their time, knowledge, and expertise. True professionals, each of them. You'll get to know them better when reach the interviews, and you will be inspired, I'm sure.

To the current crew I work with—Frank Gosch, Dan Cohen, Sohier Hall, Mike Polson, Tracey Woods, Garth O'Brien, Asif Hassan, Reiki Saito, Kathi Villaruz, Rajesh Srivastava, Stefan Weitz, and Gunawan Herri—all I can say is thanks for the opportunity to be part of an amazing global team. The last two years of my life have been a whirlwind of knowledge fueled by the passionate intellect you possess. Humbling, exciting, and educational all at the same time, my life has been forever altered in meeting you (seriously, I moved from eastern Canada to Seattle not long after meeting these people).

To Donya Dickerson, my editor, I see the value you provide in these projects. Thanks for your help, guidance, and understanding. Joseph Berkowitz got the nod to be my developmental editor, and his help, guidance, and ideas have made a noticeable improvement. Thank you, Joseph. My final editorial influencer has been Janice Race, who's wit and wisdom has added an obvious polish to the final product. Her steady and consistent eye zoomed in on every instance where my writing became lazy. Her suggestions have done much to improve the flow and clarity of each chapter. Thank you, Janice.

Finally, thanks to Donna, my ever-loving, extremely supportive wife. I think we're due for some hiking and traveling.

If there are errors in this book, they are all mine, though, as you can no doubt understand, some information will go out of date over time.

Overview

THE MAIN PURPOSE of this book is to help you monetize your Web site. While that might sound exciting, keep in mind that it takes a lot of work to accomplish. Whether you have a small or large Web site is immaterial for this discussion—scale matters less than structure and your willingness to follow specific best practices.

Thinking about and treating your Web site as if it were a traditional bricks-and-mortar business is a solid mind-set to bring to the table. You have overhead, you need a sound structure and certain technologies to house the business, and you need to "move enough product to keep the lights on." The good news for you is that compared to a traditional business, your Web site needs only storage space on a server, maybe some databases, access to the Internet, and a payment processing system if you sell directly.

Plenty of other books delve into the "how" of setting up a Web site. This book sheds light on the nuts and bolts of systems administration and focuses more on getting users to the site and detailing what to do with them when they arrive. While we will touch on arcane bits of information pertaining to server setup, connectivity, and the like, it will only be to emphasize the point we're covering.

In short, getting your Web site live is a prerequisite for reading this book. Once you've made it into the war zone of having a Web site up and running, you'll find me parachuting in to help with how to get users in the first place, and, more important, what to do with them after you get them. The real question most people I meet ask is, "How do I get someone to buy?" There are endless versions of this question, each applicable to a slightly different situation. By exploring in detail the main paths to generating traffic and by outlining how to treat each avenue in the proper manner, you will understand the best way to increase conversion. Ultimately, it is how you treat the actual people who make up this "traffic" that will determine your success.

The main options we'll examine to develop traffic and conversions are:

- Search marketing
- Internet advertising
- Videos/Webinars
- Social networking
- E-mail
- Shopping cart refinements

Each of these areas has its own set of best practices, and users originating from each must be handled in specific ways to encourage conversions. We'll examine each option in detail and explain ways to increase conversions across all paths of traffic.

Near the end of the book we'll have a talk with some successful entrepreneurs who work online every day developing conversions from their own Web sites. If you're not sure who these people are, take a quick look on Google and see for yourself. They know a lot about how to make money, and the information and advice they give is well worth taking.

Without more rambling, let's get started!

■ ■ ■ Discoverability and the Definition of "Conversion"

"Discoverability" is probably the biggest hurdle all businesses face. Conventional stores need a good location with lots of foot traffic to keep the sales flowing. Online, the same rules apply. You need users coming to your site. It's the first step in the conversion process. No visitors equals no sales. Ensuring that your site is discoverable is critical. Defining a conversion is easy, so we'll cover that first.

A conversion is basically any action taken by a user on your Web site that establishes a relationship. It can represent a sale, a sign-up to your e-mail list, a bookmark to your Web page, or even a series of page views. Your conversion is whatever you decide it should be, based on your unique business and plans.

Being discoverable needs a bit more explanation. To ensure that users can find your Web site, you need to cover some basic steps.

■ ■ ■ Create a Worthy Web Site

While this point pertains mostly to search engine marketing, sites built to be search friendly are usually also very people friendly. By ensuring that your Web site is easy to navigate, users will be able to find products and services easily. This is not only what most users expect when transacting business, but it is also something the search engines pick up. The engines appreciate it when a site is easy to crawl, and when it's easy to find the products on the site. Search engines are also watching user reactions to Web sites. If users find your Web site via a search on an engine, that engine will watch to see how long they remain on your site. Typically, search engines aren't interested in longer visits; they're just watching for users who hit the "Back" button and leave a Web site the engine highlighted.

Engines use this as an indicator that a Web site is not fulfilling users' needs. Over time, if a trend emerges, a search engine may decrease the value it places on a Web site, lower its rankings, and thus, lessen the flow of traffic to it. The engine is not doing this because it doesn't like the Web site, per se, but in reaction to user responses. The engine's job is to deliver search results in response to a query. It's your job to ensure that the Web site you operate meets the required standards each engine sets to rank well.

■ ■ ■ Keep It Simple

If you make your site simple, users will find your products and services easily. This does not mean skimping on the latest technology and building a site from basic html code. It refers, instead, to ensuring that your Web site layout is logical—that products or services are grouped together in a rational manner. By building your site in such a way, you can lead users through it, exposing them to products and services in a pattern you can control. Users will respond by following your lead, with conversion responses in tow.

Also take the time to ensure that users can easily share your Web site with others. Often your users will be your best form of advertising. Think about this a moment. If you had a particularly good online transaction with a company, you'd heartily recommend the business to family, friends, coworkers, and others. We all like to help others solve problems or nab a great deal on something, so enable your users by making sure it's easy for them to bookmark your site. Allow them the opportunity to send someone information about your company via e-mail from your Web site. Make an effort to craft an honest, helpful e-mail that's heavy on help and light on sales pitch.

Don't skip the opportunity to gain exposure via social media. If you think social media is a fad that will play out soon, you should put this book down and get a paper route. Social media represents one of the best ways to spread news about your Web site. However, there are very clear lines you shouldn't cross in the social media world, and we'll cover them in this book. Social media is the modern-day equivalent of word-of-mouth advertising, and by including quick links to social media sites, you're making it possible for visitors to instantly share the word about your site.

■ ■ ■ Jobs the Site Must Do

Your Web site must be able to manage multiple jobs simultaneously. Like any good multitasker, it needs to be good at each thing it takes on, as any deficiency will undermine the entire site. Every Web site is capable of doing many things, and you should ensure that your site does each thing well.

A Web site needs to be an educator. It needs to be a salesperson. It should be a trusted resource. It could even be a community. By successfully balancing some or all of these jobs, your site can be a leader in your chosen area. Success online depends as much on getting traffic as it does on what you do with that traffic.

■ ■ ■ Focus Breakdown

In more than 10 years of online marketing I've learned quite a bit about what works, what doesn't, and what approaches are suitable in specific situations. Based on my experience, I'm going to break down the main points in this book in order of importance. Keep in mind: this ranked order is based on the idea of generating conversions, on what I know has worked for me in the past.

1. Search marketing
2. Internet advertising
3. Videos/Webinars
4. Social networking
5. E-mail

It's important to remember that this order of importance is flexible. If your budget is tight, you may opt to pursue only one avenue. Even if you have the budget to engage in more than one form of marketing, you may decide to keep the cash in the bank and follow one or two lower-cost avenues to see how things work out before investing further. The good news is that this list can be used as a starting point and refined on your end as progress dictates.

In our first chapter we'll explore search marketing, both organic and paid. Search marketing is often the first place marketers turn, simply because it's the first place most users start looking for information. Search engines are where information seekers, shoppers, and businesses all go to find what they're looking for.

1

Search Marketing Overview: The Essentials

BEFORE WE GO INTO the specifics of how to convert people visiting your site into paying customers, it's important to have some background knowledge on search marketing.

Search marketing follows two distinct paths: search engine optimization and paid search campaigns. You can build your site around the concept of SEO (search engine optimization) and work to develop traffic via the search engines. Organic search campaigns typically have much lower costs and tend to yield results over a longer period of time. Indeed, you could view organic search marketing (also known as search engine optimization) as an initial investment of time and effort that pays dividends for years down the road. The benefits to the business are obvious, as this pipeline of traffic and conversions is virtually self-fulfilling once set up.

On the other hand, you can also employ paid search programs as a meaningful way to develop traffic. Paid search campaigns allow you to buy traffic directly from the search engines. Because there is more direct cost involved in these campaigns, most practitioners are focused specifically on driving sales. But while the cost can vary from only a few dollars a month to the millions, it is well worth exploring this "hard cost" option for marketing your products or services. Organic search campaigns typically have much lower costs and yield results over a longer period of time. As noted, SEO will eventually pay dividends.

A well-planned and well-balanced search marketing plan will include both organic and paid campaigns, as users respond differently to each option depending on where they are in their search for a product or service. As search marketing evolved, the one-site-to-do-it-all approach had to be modified to remain up-to-date. This does not mean you must build multiple Web sites, but rather that you need to carefully tailor sections of your Web site to achieve different goals.

The concept of the sales funnel will be familiar to many as an illustration of consumer buying behavior (see Figure 1.1). If you think of the typical sales funnel, "research" appears near the top of the funnel, with the transaction happening near the bottom. Organic search marketing fulfills a need near the top of this funnel and paid search marketing fulfills a need near the bottom. Many times this distinction will be blurred. To fulfill users' needs we must be able to give them the data they need during their research phase, and give them the products they decide to purchase during the transactional phase of their journey.

It makes sense to guide users through your site with proper design and well-laid-out navigation and site architecture. In this way you can include cues to the sale along the way, positively reinforcing their choice to visit your site. There is a bit of psychology at work here, as your goal should be to build trust first, then suggest the sale second. In today's age of spam Web sites, online fraud, and identity theft, users are more careful than ever with whom they choose to do business online. If you build your site correctly, you will begin building trust with them from their first visit. This trust is what will close the first and many other transactions.

■ ■ ■ The Sales Funnel

Let's examine the sales funnel in terms of organic and paid search marketing and see where each fits into the process. The path to a conversion usually begins when the user has identified a need or want. The next step is to research a solution, which in many cases leads to the purchase of an item or service. Organic search and paid search fit in at very different points on the research curve.

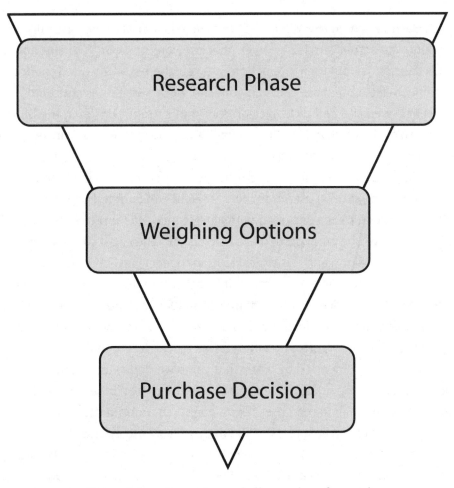

Figure 1.1. Search and the sales funnel

Early in the process, users are seeking to understand how best to fill their needs or wants, and they need to learn more. This is where organic search plays a role in the process. It is also where your efforts at being ranked well via organic search marketing can pay huge dividends. When users are directed to your Web site from a search engine, it is your first opportunity to leave a good impression.

The next layer in the purchase funnel is decision making. This layer is usually more refined than the broader research performed earlier. Your efforts to provide deep, rich content relevant to the users' search will pay off with them turning to you as a resource in this research phase. This is where your attention to detail will pay off. Users returning to a Web site at this stage in a sales funnel are much closer to making the actual purchase. Given that they are on your Web site now and already feel good about their interaction with you, there is a very good chance they will simply make a purchase through your site. At this stage it is critical to have a well-refined Web site and a clear, clean checkout system. Dropping the ball now by having a convoluted or difficult-to-follow shopping cart process will delay or kill the immediate purchase intention.

The final phase in the sales funnel is the purchase itself. This is where your paid search campaign will drive users from direct searches on targeted keywords through to specific landing pages designed with clear, concise, action-oriented verbiage. These pages have one purpose: to make conversions. They exist solely to serve your paid search campaigns, and it is critical to monitor each version that you have created. Different pages will exist to serve different search queries and to target individual products or services. It's important to monitor each landing page individually to ensure that you are running only landing pages, which convert optimally. At this stage in the sales funnel, the user's intent is very clear: it is to make a purchase.

While it is recommended by many that you have dedicated landing pages for your paid search campaigns, it is not a necessity. There is an inherent cost involved with creating and maintaining these extra pages. Thoughtful design of your original Web site pages can ensure that sales messages are incorporated into the main pages of the Web site itself. Though somewhat less effective than a dedicated landing page—depending on your Web site layout and actual targeted goals (selling product versus services, for example)—this may make more sense.

The sales funnel itself, while usually broken out into multiple phases, can easily see a user transitioning from research to purchase in a matter of minutes. Making sure you are optimized for organic search and paid search and ensuring that your Web site hits the high notes and uses best practices from each discipline will bring success in both areas—and could make a difference between success and failure.

■ ■ ■ Keyword Research

Keyword research is the best place to start any online project. When users perform a search online, they are indicating intent. Tools exist that can help you uncover the volume of queries performed by customers on a given phrase. Knowing how many potential customers are searching on a particular keyword gives you insight into potential opportunities. If the number is high, it's a good keyword to target. If the number is low, the opposite may be true.

By doing keyword research early on, you will discover exactly what your potential users are searching for. You will gain insight into the minds and intentions of your users, and this is invaluable when it comes to understanding how to best convert a visitor into a sale. You can then use this keyword research to help plan your content, your domain name purchases, your plans on where to advertise, and your paid search campaigns. Proper keyword research will help you understand the volume of searches on particular keywords and help you gauge user intent prior to investing in building your Web site.

This work is so important and valuable that it is considered the cornerstone of all online marketing projects. By this I mean it is where you should begin prior to developing anything.

Available Tools

There are a number of tools available to help you complete your keyword research projects. Some are free, while you must pay for others. In choosing a tool, it is important to understand your business's needs. It is also important to understand the cycles within your business area or vertical. If your Web site sells holiday decorations, you will experience seasonal traffic that other Web sites may not. Keyword research tools that offer a snapshot with a one-month window may be enough for such a Web site. Sites offering more generalized products or nonseasonal items will want a broader view.

Let's examine some keyword research tools and outline their basic traits.

Wordtracker

Wordtracker (www.wordtracker.com) allows you to perform keyword research and has the ability to create projects within which to catalog your research. This will allow you to easily track multiple phrase groups for different sections of your site, or track different keyword groups for multiple individual Web sites. Wordtracker also allows you to export the data, which is very useful. One downside, though, is that Wordtracker is still hamstrung by the fact it looks back only 30 days. Better than nothing, but not as powerful as Trellian's Keyword Discovery tool.

Keyword Discovery

Keyword Discovery (www.keyworddiscovery.com/index.html) is my first-line go-to research tool for new projects. It costs some money but is well worth checking out if you're serious about running your Web site as a business. The KD system looks at roughly the past 12 months' worth of search data from all the major engines (according to Keyword Discovery). This scope alone affords Keyword Discovery a much better look at what's popular with searchers over the long term. KD includes lists to save data, the ability to export data, and so on. The ability to access search query volume data through Trellian's own database makes it a powerful tool for international users. It also allows enough of a look to understand where seasonal trends lie, and it will provide a suggestion as to how many times phrases are likely to be searched daily, based on the historic data.

Another useful feature of Keyword Discovery is that it breaks down keywords focused on verticals, such as automotive, sports, recreation, arts, cooking, and more. So, if your Web site targets a specific vertical—say, automotive—KD offers insight into the top searched-on phrases for the vertical. This is an excellent way to start deeper keyword research to find hidden areas to target.

Just remember that although good tools cost money, that doesn't mean you *must* have them. Successful sites have been started using nothing but free tools and marketing techniques. You can do the same and then, as revenue grows, purchase the tools to dig deeper and continue your growth.

AdWords and adCenter

Google's AdWords and Bing's adCenter systems both incorporate tools that query volume for any given phrase. Each of these tools offers insight based on the advertising platforms their search engines use. What you see is data pulled directly from their own systems, which track every interaction they have with users.

Just remember that this data is pulled from the side of the system that deals with paid advertising. This means the data is skewed toward people whose intent was more purchase oriented as opposed to research oriented. While that may fall in line with your goals to generate conversions, it can sometimes lead you astray when developing other areas of your Web site. For example, if you create content around a keyword that drives a lot of conversions through paid search, and your plan is to monetize the page with ads, you may be surprised to see that users who take action on paid search ads don't necessarily click on ads. Clicking the paid search ad will bring them to the page but, recalling the sales funnel and the fact they are further along the purchase path, they are less interested in anything that distracts from the intent to purchase.

One great benefit of the query volume data you might get in a paid search is the ability to use what have proven to be high conversion words or phrases in your page titles. These are the actual phrases that users clicked on in an ad that you've seen convergence around. If you're running paid campaigns, this data is invaluable. While it's still true that users interacting with organic and paid search have slightly different methodologies around their interactions with your Web site, knowing which phrases develop actual conversions is a very strong indicator, which you can follow. Even if you're not running paid search campaigns, the tools provided by AdWords and adCenter can help get you started in the right direction.

Hittail.com

Another tool that can get you started in the correct direction is www.hittail.com. It provides real-time insight into data around which keywords customers used in queries that that led them to your Web site. Easy to install, this is a great tool for those who want to dive deep into this type of data.

More Ways to Find Keywords to Target

The following are additional ways to find more keywords:

- Look at internal searches—examine "failed" searches
- Google Insights
- Google Trends
- Google AdWords tool—no date range limitation
- Google Suggest—in search box drop-down
- www.icerocket.com—monitors blogs and social media trending

- www.scoutlabs.com
- www.twitter.com home page lists current trends data
- www.seoquake.com toolbar
- www.enquisite.com can track conversion rates for targeted keywords and help estimate the amount of time versus ROI (return on investment) on an SEO project
- SEOmoz Linkscape: www.seomoz.org/linkscape

This chapter was designed to cover some of the basic topics involved with search marketing. We paid particular attention to keyword research, as all search marketing efforts revolve around keywords that users type into a search engine. It is therefore critical that you have a firm understanding of what those users are looking for so you can target your efforts to match their requests.

The next chapter will guide you through how to perform search engine optimization. We'll also cover the main points you'll need to manage on your Web site. We're putting time into this topic because, for many Web sites, traffic from search engines can account for over 75 percent of overall inbound traffic, so getting SEO right can have a profound impact on gaining users who can be converted later. The more traffic you have, the greater the chance to convert.

2

Performing Organic Search Marketing: Driving Low-Cost Traffic

SINCE THE ADVENT OF search engines, businesses have looked for ways to gain favor with the engines and attract more traffic. Today, search engines may represent upward of 40, 50, 60, or even 70 percent or more of a Web site's inbound referrals. Ideally, search engines, such as Bing and Google, will find your information online and bring it to the attention of potential customers. Having said that, you should make an effort to ensure that your Web site is as optimized as possible so your customers can easily find you.

Each search engine has a unique crawler or robot whose job is to uncover the content you have on your Web site. If you keep in mind that these crawlers are seeking information in much the same way a user would, it is easy to understand the importance of optimizing your Web site to be crawled easily. The main difference between robots and any other user, though, is how simple these robots are in their approach. They will have neither Flash nor JavaScript enabled; they cannot see text in your images; and, obviously, they cannot understand the relationship of content as humans can.

The relationship between human users and robot users is important to understand. While robots are linear in their approach to visiting your Web site, humans move around randomly. A search engine spider will begin with the first link it finds on your Web site, and it will continue to crawl each and every additional link it finds. By doing so, the crawler can access all of the content available to it. If the crawler does not have JavaScript enabled, it will not be able to follow links found within its JavaScript-held content. In such an example the crawler would have a very limited view of the Web site, and, as a consequence, would miss out on indexing portions of your Web site. Getting indexed is the first step to ranking well. And to clarify a point for you, the terms "search engine crawler," "crawler," "spider," and "robot" all refer to the same thing and can be used interchangeably. They all refer to the tool run by a search engine whose job is to visit your Web site and bring back information about your site to the engines themselves.

When humans—as opposed to our robot friends, the crawlers—view your Web site, they follow very different patterns. They are influenced by your site's layout, ad placements, offers for other items or services, and by their unique needs. The search engines are concerned with your site presenting useful content to a user, as opposed to caring about how a user navigates your Web site.

Each time a search engine sends users to your Web site, it watches that transaction for details that can help it understand the value of your site. If users come into your Web site, navigate it easily, and find what they want quickly and with minimal effort, they will stay longer and be more likely to revisit. If, on the other hand, the links are obscurely named, it's difficult for users to find something, their time is wasted by slow loading, they'll hit the "Back" button quickly. It's extremely important to remember that these users asked the engine to supply them the best results for their query, and your Web site came up.

The engine is always looking to improve its results, and, again, by watching how long users spend on your site, it picks up clues on the value users place on the site. Multiply one user by thousands, or even millions, sent to your site and these "value reports" paint a telling picture for the engine. If enough users simply click the "Back" after entering your site and looking around briefly, the search engine will begin to alter the value it places on that site (usually with a lower ranking). The net result is less traffic from the search engine to your site.

That small circle of events illustrates one of the over 200 factors the typical search engine algorithm includes. Those algorithms are very closely guarded secrets by the engines. Only a few people at the engines themselves even have access to the entire algorithmic string, so we are left to guess what actually does matter. By "guess," though, we mean "test." With over a decade of practice in the books, professional search engine optimizers have learned a lot about how to build a Web site that will rank well in the search results served by the engines. Many billions of dollars are spent by businesses each year in the quest to develop more inbound traffic from the search engines.

There are certain best practices you should follow in the world of search engine optimization, which we will discuss in detail. Taking these measures is probably one of the best ways to direct traffic to your Web site while limiting the monetary investment you need to make, so it's critical we explore this in some depth.

■ ■ ■ Domain Name

There is much debate over what makes a domain name great, but everyone agrees on the basics. A short, memorable name is preferable. You can coin a new word or phrase, or choose from the almost endless possibilities that already exist in our vocabulary. Though there are a lot of options, don't make the mistake of assuming that the domain you want is available. "Domaining" is a popular way to make money, in which a person buys a domain and then resells it for more money at a later time. Very few if any single words in the English language remain available in the *.com* TLD (Top Level Domain, the highest ranking domains in the Domain Name System). When searching for a domain that is still available, look beyond the *.com* variants and explore options around other TLDs such as *.net* and *.org*.

The *.org* domains tend to be less business focused and more service oriented. While you can easily set up a site to sell products or services on an *.org*, most sites using this TLD tend toward informational services, as opposed to sales. Many do actually sell products or services, but they do so as a logical extension of the informational services they provide. An *.org* about surfing, for example, might be tracking wave activity at popular surf spots as a service to the surfing community. It may also show ads for products surfers use, such as board wax, as this is a logical tie-in.

In reality, though, the *.com* remains king. People all over the world have been trained to type in *.com* after any Web site name, so having the *.com* is the best way to go. Getting the right *.com* for your site might cost you, though, since someone might already own the one you want. Even though some *.com* domains have sold for seven figures in recent years, most transactions happen at a fraction of that. Often the domain you want can be had for a few hundred dollars. If you can afford it, grab it. If not, don't fret, simply choose another domain.

■ ■ ■ ONLINE RESOURCE ■ ■ ■

New TDLs are introduced every so often; the current crop can be found by visiting the ICAAN Web site. Internet Corporation for Assigned Names and Numbers is the official governing body for domains. Check out this link for the most current list of TLDs: www.icann.org/en/registries/top-level-domains.htm

■ ■ ■ Site Structure: Technical SEO

In this section we'll cover things such as content location (how to structure your site), URL structure (what the folder structure looks like and the importance of having a clean URL), more technical SEO points (which items should be included, such as H1 tags, as opposed to what to write in them), and site navigation. It's best to think of all of these points as somewhat related, as each has a bearing on or is influenced by the others. Let's dive in with a quick checklist you can keep handy to use on your own site construction or redesign.

Content Location

Your site's structure has a lot to do with your success in search marketing. How you lay out your Web site tells the search engines which content you value. Your users will also pick up on these subtle cues, so taking the time to structure your Web site logically will pay dividends in search engine optimization and in user satisfaction.

In terms of SEO, you want to ensure that your content stays near the root of the domain. Simply put, keep your content as close to the home page as possible. We've all been to Web sites that require us to delve through four or five layers to finally find what we're after. By making users click ever deeper into the Web site, you risk losing them. After all, a user's main focus is the product itself, not figuring out where you placed it in your Web site. If you make users think too much, they will simply hit the "Back" button and leave your site for the next one in the search engine's list of results.

You should focus on grouping content together in a logical way, so users can easily follow the navigation and reach their goal. Do not let the limitations of a particular piece of software or an application stand in the way. Use a different system if needed, but make sure the structure—and thus the navigation—is easy to follow. For the search engines, you should limit folder depths on your own Web site to less than four from the home page. On your own Web site, this would resemble the following sample URL:

www.domain.come/folder-1/folder-2/folder-3/folder-4/file-name.html

In such an example, we are telling search engines the content to be found there is less important than the content found in the first three folder levels, and much less important than the content found on the home page. Keep this subtle distinction in mind. From the users' point of view, this might be the difference between their staying on your Web site or leaving it. Remember, making users work too hard to find something usually results in their leaving the Web site.

URL Structure

Also important in the discussion of structure are the individual, discrete URLs that constitute the actual locations for each piece of content you produce. Too often the URL structure is overlooked when building a site or setting one up on new software. This is another area where we can face some big limits to our ability to reach an optimized product.

While the search engine crawlers have come a long way in their abilities to crawl and ingest content, they can still have trouble negotiating overly long or complex URLs. By placing such URL structures in front of search engine crawlers, you force them to use more resources to find your content. Keep this up long enough and all the crawlers will turn to your competition instead.

Let's take a look at proper URL structure. First, in Figure 2.1, you will see the search performed and search result returned:

Search: Space shuttle *Atlantis*
Result:

Photo of **Space Shuttle Atlantis** & Hubble **Space** Telescope …
Related Posts: - A Giant Spider Attacks **Space Shuttle Atlantis**. - NASA Astronaut Mark Polansky Will Be Posting To Twitter Live From The **Space Shuttle** …
laughingsquid.com/photo-of-space-shuttle-atlantis-hubble-space-telescope-transiting-the-sun/ -
Cached - Similar - 💬 ⤒ ✗

Figure 2.1. Space shuttle search

In the above example you can see that the clean, search-friendly URL is keyword rich; that is, it's filled with words that concisely describe the content, without any additional characters. The goal should be for each URL to contain some of the exact keywords that users will type into the search engine. If your URL is clean and has those keywords in it, you can increase your visible footprint in the engine's search results. This is very helpful in attracting the attention of users while they scan the results page for an item to click on. Compare that first example with the one in Figure 2.2. Note that in this second example the URL is not as clean:

Search: Panasonic Lumix digital camera
Result:

Panasonic Lumix DMC-**FZ18K** Digital Camera - **Yahoo! Shopping**
Yahoo! Shopping is the best place to comparison shop for **Panasonic** Lumix DMC-**FZ18K** -
Digital Camera. Compare products, compare prices, read reviews and …
shopping.yahoo.com/p:Panasonic%20Lumix%20DMC-FZ18K%20Digital%
20Camera:**1994886551** - 16 hours ago - Cached - Similar -

Figure 2.2. Panasonic search

In this second example we start to see some of the subtle deviations from this formula. If the original programming includes spaces, the result is a bunch of "%20" notations that clutter up your URL. You will need to account for spaces between words in your URL, and the best way to manage this is to use hyphens as word spacers (as in the first example). The hyphen has always been a recognized word separator, whereas the underscore, previously a popular separator, has fallen out of favor. Even though it's not a complete dead end for the crawlers, the difference between the clean and not-so-clean URLs makes a difference to search engines.

While setting up your Web site, it's helpful to perform some detailed keyword research to understand which words and phrases users actually search for in relation to your site's product. This research will uncover the volume of queries made on individual phrases or words, helping you figure out what is most popular for any given topic. By using those popular phrases and words in your URL structure, you place the words in a position to be bolded in the search results, which helps to attract the searcher's eye to your listing.

One final item to note is whether to capitalize words in a URL. I'll keep this simple: don't. Any time you capitalize a word in a URL, you create the possibility for duplication of content. Crawlers (and most servers) see each version of the URL as valid and individual. No sense creating extra work for yourself and the engines by allowing duplicate pages to exist on your Web site. Stick with all lowercase letters in your URLs.

Technical SEO

There are some basic elements you want to be sure to cover if you are optimizing your Web site. These items are considered technical in nature only because the references are to elements generally hidden inside the code of a Web page. Let's examine them from the top down.

Doctype

The doctype refers to the type of coding used by a page. As defined by the W3C (World Wide Web Consortium), the doctype declaration should be the very first thing in an HTML document, before the <html> tag. The doctype declaration is not an HTML tag; it is an instruction to the Web browser about what version of the markup language the page is written in. The doctype declaration refers to a Document Type Definition. The DTD specifies the rules for the markup language so that browsers can render the content correctly.

■ ■ ■ ONLINE RESOURCE ■ ■ ■

There are various declarations or "doctypes" that are applicable to individual types of markup languages. It's useful to read the following Web page to fully understand these items: www.w3schools.com/tags/tag_DOCTYPE.asp

Page Title

It is critical to get this item right when optimizing your Web site. Your title tells the search engines what the topic of the page is. A Web site with content about apples might have a page titled "Red Delicious Apples—Growing and Harvesting." It's the first place the search engines encounter keywords to associate with your content. The title of each and every page on your Web site should be unique and discrete. You should have only one title per page, as well. Keep those keywords you want to be found when a user searches up front too. And try to keep the overall length of the title to around 65 characters. If you need to go longer, that's fine, just be sure to place those targeted keywords up front and inside those first 65 characters.

Meta Description

This item will test your skills. Write a relevant, keyword-rich, targeted meta description, and your reward is that Google will use it as the description shown in the search results when your page is shown to a searcher. Miss the mark in Google's eyes, and the searcher will scan your Web page for some content it thinks represents the page and use that. This outcome should be avoided at all costs, as you know what the page is about better than Google does. The engine is taking a guess, and usually it's inaccurate. Ever done a search and seen what looks like a series of random words in the description? That's a clue that the Web site either got its meta description wrong or it didn't have one at all.

Sometimes the phrases and text that show up on a search engine to describe a Web site, while appearing to be a coherent string, are in fact a collection of random items plucked from a page by the engine and placed together to resemble a description. If you viewed the source code of such a page, you'd notice a lack of meta description in the code. Nada. This forced the engine to cull content from the page in order to build the page itself.

Limit the meta description to 150 characters or so and place your targeted keywords for the page's content as close to the beginning of this information as possible. The text should be grammatically correct and not repeat the targeted keywords needlessly. Ensure that each meta description is unique to the page it will appear on, and keep each meta description crisply relevant to only the content on that page. If you cannot fill in the meta description tag, leave it empty instead of using a generic, repetitive tag across multiple pages, which should only be a last resort.

Meta Keywords

Take the time to fill these in correctly. Use relevant keywords and even a few common misspellings if you like. You can include up to 25 words or phrases, with each word or phrase separated by commas. The finished product would look something like this: "keyword, keyword, two-word phrase, keyword, keewoord" (keyword misspelled). The engines don't place a lot of value on this tag, but getting it right shows you are interested in presenting a properly maintained Web site in front of the engines. This speaks to the quality of your product in other areas. The main thing to remember about meta keywords is to not overdo it. Don't add extra words, and don't use words unrelated to the content on the page.

H Tags

Commonly referred to as H tags, heading tags are a way to indicate to users and search engines the main focus of the content on a page. When we read a newspaper or a book, we need signposts so we can understand which chapters we're in and which paragraphs we're reading. "Headings" are a common way to make these delineations obvious to readers. On a Web site, these tags help us place signposts to alert users and search engines to what we're talking about. Generally these tags are used when setting style for different areas of the Web page.

We can use these tags to illustrate to the search engines the importance of select keywords on a page. By placing the keywords we want to target within the H1 tag, we demonstrate to the search engine the importance of this phrase or keyword in relation to the content of the page. The H1 section, for example, would highlight the main theme of the page area. The H2 through H6 tags would appear lower on the page as a way to guide us into new areas on the same topic.

These tags further reinforce the topic by using related keywords to aid migration through the content of a given page. When composing H tags, you should choose synonyms for the keyword as opposed to using the keyword over and over. Obviously there will be times when repeating the keyword is necessary, so a good rule of thumb is to read all of your content aloud. If it sounds normal, it's fine for the search engines.

Image ALT Tags

With universal search more and more often showing blended results, spending time optimizing your images is an excellent way to increase your inbound traffic. The concept of universal search is illustrated when you see news, video, images, and the rest of the normal results (the 10 blue links typically seen at Google) returned on the search engine results page (SERP). Figure 2.3 shows a sample of universal search in action at Google. Note the images, text links, and video the searcher sees.

The images across the top of the SERP page are capable of driving large amounts of traffic to each of the Web sites that host them. By ensuring that the images are properly optimized by using keyword-rich, relevant descriptive ALT tags, these Web sites are enjoying direct traffic from these images. While their own Web pages may not rank as well, these images are doing the trick for the Web sites that own the images and are driving in traffic just the same.

When naming your images, take the time to clearly describe what is actually in them. Use relevant, related keywords. It is through this description that search engines will understand what your images are about. Search engines do not view images as you and I do. We see pictures and understand what they represent. Search

| jeep srt8 | Search | Advanced Search |
| | | Preferences |

Image results for **jeep srt8** - Report images

Jeep – 2009 **Jeep** Grand Cherokee – Features – **SRT8**
Official 2009 Jeep Grand Cherokee site. The 09 Jeep Grand Cherokee SRT8 combines 4WD
capability with Street and Racing Technology. Learn more.
www.jeep.com/en/2009/grand_cherokee/exterior/srt8/ - Cached – Similar

YouTube – **Jeep SRT8** vs ML 63 AMG from inside the ML 63 AMG
34 sec – Apr 14, 2007 - ★★★★☆
BMW 335i vs 650 vs **Jeep SRT8** vs MB S600 vs 911 vs Audi S8 … **Jeep** Grand
Cherokee **SRT-8** Full Throtle 0-190 kph in Kuwait …
www.youtube.com/watch?v-epmGE--EtN0

Review: 2009 Jeep Grand Cherokee SRT8—Autoblog
Mar 16, 2009 … The Jeep SRT8 gets visual and functional enhancements inside and out, turning
this off-road animal into a true street performance machine. …
www.autoblog.com/.../review-2009-**jeep**-grand-cherokee-**srt98**/ - Cached – Similar

Figure 2.3. Jeep search

engines must use other cues and clues to understand what the images represent. Effective naming and effective use of the ALT tag will ensure that search engines understand what your images depict. Getting these details correct is an excellent way to drive to your Web site users who are in the early research phase of a purchase.

Don't worry if you are showing the same image that many other Web sites are showing. A picture of a watch for sale is a picture of a watch for sale. It will be the same watch that is for sale no matter whose Web site it is on. It is very important to take the time to optimize your images, as they can bring in a significant portion of your traffic. Optimized images can give you an edge on your competition, leading to more visitors and higher conversion rates.

■ ■ ■ Content

The actual content on your Web site will be determined more or less by the topic or product(s) you are focused on. A broader focus allows for more content, while a niche view narrows your options. Broad is not necessarily the way forward, however. The Internet has been around for a while now, so the "go broad" approach has already been done and done again, with the biggest players firmly entrenched in their leading positions. It would be possible to knock one of them off, but it's unlikely. A more likely path to success is to stay focused in a narrower field. Lest you think it's all been done before, a lot of opportunity still exists if you choose your focal point and dig deeply into it.

I mentioned keyword research earlier, and the value of that research will show in this phase of site planning as well. By reviewing your keyword research, you will see the words and phrases specifically related to your product or topic that users are actively seeking content on. Back to our example of a Web site selling watches: if your keyword research shows users looking for a particular brand of watch, or an accessory for a watch such as a new strap, clearly, you should have content to match their need.

If you create pages with little content on them, the value of those pages to the search engines is greatly diminished. Creating pages of content that are at least 250 words in depth ensures that the search engines will see the site as a legitimate one, and one with usable content to offer visitors. However, the search engines are not interested in showing search results of pages that contain basically the same content. They want unique results. This is where the real work of building and maintaining a Web site comes in. Your job is to create unique content for each page. You can do so by writing the content yourself or by paying others to write it for you. One truth remains, though: the content has to be yours alone, and neither taken from nor displayed anywhere else. Someone must sit down and write it.

Once you've begun generating content—250 words to a page—make sure that you have it spread out over enough pages so that readers will be able to stay on your Web site for a while. Your site should start out with at least 10 pages of unique content. You could live with fewer pages if your content is strong enough, but your goal should be to create at least 100 pages of content as quickly as possible. Having 100 pages will illustrate to the engines that your site has some depth to it—they will know that you are bringing a useful amount of content to the Web. Trying to compete against established Web sites with only 15 to 20 pages will result in disappointment, as your site will simply not have the weight needed to compete and rank well. While this rule is not an absolute, I can tell you from experience that the more unique content you add to your site, the better it performs. Users respond to the "authority" of a well-developed and content-rich Web site by linking to it. The engines see this linking and respond by ranking you better, starting the cycle all over again.

Where does this rule leave folks using feeds of content from other sources, such as RSS feeds, for content, or those with e-commerce Web sites housing tens of thousands of products? Well, it seems to leave them in a tough spot. The best practice will not be changed, simply because it would be a lot of work to write unique content. Thankfully, however, there exists a gray area. While we talk in terms of creating unique content, the reality is that each *page* must be unique. Semantics you say? Nope. Just fact.

To you and me, content is generally the written words appearing on a Web page, although it also includes the images, videos, comments, and other visual elements we see. This definition of content is accurate, but the search engines' crawlers take it to a much deeper level. Because they don't view a page as humans do—as a mixture of the text and visual elements—they have a very particular, narrow view of what content is. They view the *code* as the content. Each character represents something to a crawler, and those characters, when combined, form instructions to the Web browser we use to surf the Internet. When the browser executes those commands, you and I see the images, text videos, and so on. The crawler, however, will only see the code.

And herein lies the way to differentiate your Web site from another using substantially the same content. While both sites may have posted the same article on a news topic, for example, the physical layouts of the sites will differ. These kinds of differences translate into differences between the code of each Web site and Web page. That difference matters to the crawlers because they understand that even though the text on the page—the actual words—may be the same, the sites are individual. If you can do a solid job of mixing your feed-sourced content with elements that make your site and pages more unique, the overall effect will be a Web site that appears "substantially unique."

Now, to make sure your head is screwed on correctly around this point once and for all, the best practice is to make/create content for your Web site that is significantly different from that of your competitors'. The days of creating Web sites featuring purely feed-derived content and seeing those sites rank well in the engines are over. Too many people have exploited this idea, and the engines have responded with deeper filtering. I mention this tactic simply as an example of what has been attempted and what no longer works. Feed-derived content is not a cure-all for a Web site lacking unique content.

■ ■ ■ An Editorial Plan

You should set up and organize an editorial plan for your content. It does not matter if you sell individual products and services or if you simply monetize your Web site through advertising related to your content. An effective, well-thought-out, and well-executed editorial plan will help you build content that attracts users, encourages them to link to the content, and facilitates a sale. Ensuring that your content is unique and keyword-rich will drive search engines to frequently visit your site, index it deeply, and showcase your pages when a user makes a specific search related to a topic you cover. It may seem like a lot of effort because it is. Running a Web site is like running any other business: it takes work to be successful.

For many this work includes the creation of unique content to showcase on the Web site. You can easily lay out an editorial plan that will help you successfully cover all areas related to your Web site's topic, ensuring a deep, rich experience for users coming to your site from the search engines. An easy way to accomplish this feat is by using the flash cards you might use to make short notes for doing presentations. Creating an editorial plan this way allows you to visualize your Web site by laying out each page on paper. By labeling each one from the home page on down through the main areas of the Web site, and to each individual Web page itself, you will get a sensible layout depth and breadth of the Web site and its content. You will now also have a better idea of all the work you'll have to do. At this point your goal is to begin creating content for each of these items.

If you have a Web site focused on e-commerce, creating an editorial plan may be less involved. Your aim should be to plan the basic structure of the Web site, while stopping short of laying out a notepaper for each and every product (anyone else beneath your roof would probably balk at seeing that much notepaper stuck to all the walls). By taking the time to complete this exercise, you will be able to understand the various areas of your Web site and see how to best organize all of your content.

To ensure the continual growth of your Web site, you should set up a basic editorial calendar. Whether you're selling products, services, or simply allowing free access to your content, you need to determine on which dates you will roll out your new content. It is the consistency of posting this new content on your Web site that keeps users and search engines returning.

A basic editorial calendar may be as simple as a notation on your calendar in the kitchen at home. The goal is to create a system that reminds you when to produce new content. You will figure out which content to focus on and when to produce it through continual keyword research and by testing your own Web site. By watching how users interact with your current content, you can gain insights into how you can better refine your product or service offering.

It's important to remember that while you will have to put effort into growing your Web site, you can work efficiently to create the content you need. In the case of a Web site that has content pages monetized through advertising placements, such as a simple blog, posting new content three or four times a week will keep the cycle moving. A service-oriented Web site could also be built around a simple blog, and the resulting site used to communicate to potential users. If yours is an e-commerce Web site, you should be continually expanding the descriptions of your products, because the repetitive product descriptions shown by all other Web sites using the same product source will hurt your chances for success. By investing the time in rewriting these descriptions to be richer and more detailed, you will ensure that users respond by frequenting your Web site and purchasing through you as opposed to others.

Building Links

Building links is one of the most important things you will do for your Web site. The goal of building links is always twofold. First, you want to get traffic. Giving users of Web sites that already receive a lot traffic the option to follow a link to your site will bring a small amount of the established site's traffic over your way. The second goal is to help elevate your site in the eyes of the search engines. When other Web sites link to yours, it's a vote of confidence from them; they have vouched for your legitimacy. The search engines look specifically for this linking activity and use it to help rate your site. By collecting links from reputable, quality sites, your own site is seen as more important, more authoritative, more trustworthy.

One key thing to keep in mind is that building links should be done with an eye for quality, not quantity. It is far better to have a single link from a well-ranked Web site rather than 10 links from poorly ranked sites. If we speak in Googlese, it's the Page Rank that matters most for this conversation. Page Rank (PR) is Google's way of representing the value it places on a Web site or individual page. While PR is important, you shouldn't chase it; rather, use it as a guide to help you target the Web sites you'd like to ask for a link. While most of the engines have their own version of this rating system, Google's is most obvious, as it publishes the data openly.

Even though Google's Page Rank information is acknowledged to be several months old at any given time, it's useful for understanding the relative value of sites from which to request links when doing side-by-side comparisons. For this same reason, because the data from Google is old, you should conduct your due diligence and carefully examine those sites from which you want to request links. Also, given the age of this data, it should be treated as a trend, not an absolute. Gaining links from Web sites viewed as dubious by the search engines will lead to your own site being viewed with suspicion. Sites that typically are rated well by Google's own Page Rank data are often well regarded, though, thus the Page Rank data is a good place to start your search when requesting links. An even simpler measure of the value of the Web site from which you want to request a link is how well the site ranks in searches. If it ranks well, there's a good chance it is a trusted site and worth the request.

Managing the links from your own Web site to other sites is just as important, though, so spare some time to choose carefully who you link out to. Choosing the wrong sites to link to from your own Web site can sink a Web site in a very short time. If, for example, you choose to place a link to a site that installs malware or spyware on a user's computer, you will not be highly regarded by the search engines.

At this point you might be inclined to panic. What if a bad Web site simply posts a link to your Web site? Will you be hurt by this? Largely, no. The search engines are looking for trends. If enough links from bad Web sites accumulate and are pointed at your Web site, then yes, that would hurt your rankings and success. If only a few point at you, however, you'll still be fine.

Bottom line, carefully choose those from whom to request links and don't sweat what you cannot control, such as who links to you of their own choice.

Getting the links isn't easy either. In fact, even in the age of the Internet, one of the best means of getting links is to contact Web site owners/operators directly and request the links. The trick is finding those owners/operators. Given the sheer volume of people online, most well-ranked Web sites receive loads of inbound e-mail and contact requests. Most of those items end up unanswered, so making your request through normal channels is often not the best route (although it *is* an avenue you should pursue).

I've had success with the following process:

1. Find a direct contact name/e-mail.
2. Craft an open, honest note.
3. Prove you are a real person by providing your full name and contact information and saying when you're available to chat, if the contact would like to do so.
4. Take the work out of it for the contact—include in your note the page on which you want the link placed and give the contact the anchor text (the words to be linked) you want used.
5. Include a logical follow-up time in your note; give the contact a week or two to consider the request, then follow up again.
6. If the contact doesn't respond after your follow-up, go on to the next contact—no one likes to be spammed, and that is how your frequent e-mails will be perceived.

Of all the above suggestions, it's probably the first one that will leave you wondering: How will searching the contact page on a Web site yield an easy answer? Fortunately, legislation requires domain owners to keep accurate, up-to-date records of their contact information. While domain owners can opt to have this personal information overwritten with private information from a third party, it still leaves you with a path to explore. That path can be summed up in two words, combined to form one: WhoIs.

WhoIs information is your best bet in tracking down a human being at a Web site (see Figure 2.4). Most folks have never heard of WhoIs, and more than a few will be shocked to learn that their name, address, and phone number are freely available via this system if they own a domain (unless, as mentioned, they opt to pay a third party to use *their* information). WhoIs acts as an intermediary, passing along any requests for contact to the actual domain owners, while shielding their information from public view.

WhoIs information can get you a contact at a Web site from which you're looking to request a link. It might be just an administrative contact or a technical contact, but it's better than a contact link that leads nowhere, as some links tend to do. If you want a link from a good Web site, be ready to work for it. You'll still need to invest time in making contact and crafting a compelling pitch for why the site should link to you, but, from experience, I can say the approach works, and the results are worth it.

Next we'll explore some ways to convert the traffic you receive from organic search efforts. Get ready to delve deeper into the world of search marketing and also into the ways that different forms of search marketing can bring you users at different stages of the research/purchase cycle. How you treat these users will affect how successful you are in converting them into customers.

To find WhoIs information, start with www.whois.net

WHOIS information for **microsoft.com** :

```
[Querying whois.internic.net]
[Redirected to whois.tucows.com]
[Querying whois.tucows.com]
[whois.tucows.com]
Registrant:
Microsoft Corporation
One Microsoft Way
Redmond, WA 98052
US


Domain name: MICRSOFT.COM


Administrative Contact:
   Administrator, Domain domains@microsoft.com
   One Microsoft Way
   Redmond, WA 98052
   US
   ▦▾ +1.4258828080 ☾
Technical Contact:
   Hostmaster, MSN msnhst@microsft.com
   One Microsoft Way
   Redmond, WA 98052
   US
   ▦▾ +1.4258828080 ☾


Registration Service Provider:
   Melbourne IT DBS, support@melbourneitdbs.com
   ▦▾ 1-866-907-3267 ☾ (fax)
   ▦▾ 1-650-963-3266 ☾
   Please contact Melbourne IT DBS, Inc. for domain updates,
   DNS/Nameserver changes, and general domain support questions.
```

Figure 2.4. WhoIs information

3

Converting Organic Search Marketing: The Five Pillars of Trust

GIVEN THAT USERS originating from organic search are less focused on making an immediate purchase, it's important to make sure you handle them in a way that makes them comfortable. The leap from research to purchase is a big one, and many need time to think through the buying decision. A person may want to make a purchase but not be ready for a variety of reasons. Offering a gentle but guiding hand is usually the best approach for converting these folks who are on the fence. Generally speaking, it's best to assume that most users who end up on your Web site via organic search fall into this category.

Let's examine a process approach to reviewing your Web site with an eye toward pinpointing areas to focus on that will help convert this large group of organically driven users. We'll call it the Five Pillars of Trust:

- Trust 1: Authority
- Trust 2: Explanations
- Trust 3: Simplicity
- Trust 4: Follow-up
- Trust 5: Security

The goal with this exercise is to get you thinking about what matters to your users. Building trust is incredibly important because you are, in essence, asking them for very personal information, such as their addresses and credit card numbers. Users don't usually provide such information easily, so building trust with them is a critical step. If you can view the entire process through their eyes, you'll come very close to getting the process right every time.

Pillar of Trust 1: Authority

How many times have you searched for something at a major search engine online and been left flat by the result? Sure there's a picture of the item, and maybe a few words explaining it, but you really wanted multiple images, from various angles. You wanted to be able to see the item up close, to zoom right in, as if you held the item close to your face. You wanted a detailed explanation offering every possible detail about the item. Not just the basic measurements, but the weight, color options, accessories, various model numbers, and so on.

You are hoping to actually come as close as possible as you can to touching and understanding the item while remaining on your computer. Yet the result you just clicked on is showing one image and a product number. From there the Web site offers one button to add the item to your cart and check out. Hardly the ideal approach to encouraging sales.

If you take the time to incorporate multiple images (clickable to view larger, high-quality versions), to offer detailed explanations and descriptions, and generally to provide as much information about the product, service, or item as possible, you will be seen as an "authority" Web site. This distinction is critical. When a user sees your site as an authority, all others are compared to yours. By ensuring the in-depth experience on your site, users quickly refine their efforts from searching for multiple sites that can meet their needs to searching one site for the product or service they seek.

Look to eBay auctions to validate this thinking. If you track successful sellers on eBay, one thing they have in common is the appearance of being an authority. Far from simply seeming to be authorities, these sellers have established themselves as authorities. They may be solo entrepreneurs, but this does not detract from their success. Early on they learned that more images sell more products. Higher-quality images sell more products. More detailed descriptions sell more products. These successful sellers have incorporated all of these factors (and more) into their spaces. Users respond to this effort by frequenting their "stores" and buying more from them directly.

Those running service-oriented sites might want to take the approach of including testimonials on the sites. Adding testimonials from satisfied past clients builds credibility and trust with those new to a site. If users find you via a search engine result, there's every chance you are new to them, so building credibility is a balancing act between your content and what others have to say about you. Brag about the good, chase down the bad, and try to make it right. By showcasing your openness, you build trust. By showcasing thought-leading and relevant content, you demonstrate your authority on the topic at hand.

Trust leads directly to being seen as an authority. Prove you are trustworthy—to the search engines and users—and you will be viewed as an authority. Again, you want this position in the minds of both users and search engines. Authoritative Web sites rank well in search results.

Pillar of Trust 2: Explanations

Another way to build the kind of trust that results in conversions is with detailed explanations. "Detail" is the watchword here. Make sure to note every piece of information no matter how mundane or insignificant you think it might be. From detailed product descriptions to warranty and return policy information—don't skip one single thing. Take the time to uncover the most detailed information about a product and publish it on your Web site. List every facet of every service, no matter how trivial.

Be sure to watch for current trends your potential customers may want to know about. If the news has recently been focused on the issue of children's toys and products from China containing lead-based paints, and your products do not contain them, it's worth calling out. Yes, this announcement is nearly as redundant as labeling a naturally fat-free product with a sticker saying "Now Fat Free!" However, it's information like this that helps to sell the product in an increasingly crowded marketplace.

Take the time to research the common next steps and explain them to your users too. If you sell a product, they will want to know about shipping, taxes, and potential duties when crossing borders. While it may be too much work to try to keep on top of cross-border information for everyone, a series of links to useful information from the most common countries you see visitors from would help them a lot. Shipping information is probably the most commonly sought information, so integrate a postage calculator into your site. It might be worth formalizing a business relationship with the preferred shipper of your choice at this stage, as many offer such calculators for Web sites to clients. Others are available free online.

An excellent way to build trust through explanations is to keep a running list of every question posed to you by users or clients. This list can be turned into a deep FAQ (Frequently Asked Questions) list, where you state the question and list the answer. Striving to create a comprehensive FAQ is time well invested, as having answers quick at hand for your users helps them build trust by removing the barriers unanswered questions create. Don't leave any questions unanswered, and update your information to reflect new information and any successful solutions you've provided for unique questions.

■ ■ ■　Pillar of Trust 3: Simplicity

How do you showcase all the information users might want while maintaining a clean Web site and ensuring that users aren't overwhelmed? Keeping all the detail in your explanations simple is one of the toughest jobs you'll have in getting more conversions, but I'll help you do that.

First, keep the important information at the top of the page so that your users can find it immediately. More detailed information should go lower on the page, and even more detailed information lower still, and so on. The goal is to showcase, first and foremost, the actual product the users came looking for—images sell, so keep them up top.

Next, users want product descriptions and details, so that information should follow. And then they might want information such as measurements, weights, and so on, so that needs to be showcased as well.

For common details such as gift wrapping, accessories, and shipping information, you can insert a link module near the top of the page with links to individual pages rich in information for each specific topic. This makes it easy for users to locate answers to questions on obviously related topics: If I buy a gift from you, can you wrap it and ship it for me? What are the extra costs for shipping? These sorts of questions are of concern to your users, so provide the information up front. Building a common link module that appears near any of your products, items, or services is an excellent way to show users a direct path to more information, while using minimal real estate on the page and keeping things simple. In fact, keeping things simple helps build trust the old-fashioned way: it proves you have nothing up your sleeve, nothing hidden. When users shop online, they do not like surprises, so a clean presentation helps minimize confusion and keeps shoppers on track.

This trend toward simplicity should extend to your shopping cart and checkout systems as well. Building a simple site won't help if the shopping cart and checkout experience confuses your users. From the moment a user clicks on an item, the path from placing it into the shopping cart to checking out should be as short and obvious as possible. Some may argue that this is the ideal time to show a user more items in hopes of increasing the "cart load" and final checkout amount, but I say keep it simple. This doesn't mean, however, that you shouldn't experiment with the opportunity to showcase related items. You just need to do so in a thoughtful, nonintrusive way.

By now it's likely that everyone is familiar with the Amazon.com suggestion: "Readers who bought this book also purchased these similar titles." An amazingly simple and powerful bit of text. By suggesting related titles, Amazon manages to expose users to similar products, ensuring at the very least that users know Amazon has more of what they like, and, at the other end of the spectrum, directly increasing revenue through added sales. Amazon gets this right.

An example of a Web site failing at this is www.godaddy.com. Anyone who has purchased through GoDaddy is familiar with the high-pressure overload tactics designed to increase sales of items to people less than familiar with the environment. Sure, all those additional things sound like a good idea, but when your intent was to spend $7.99 on a domain name, seeing your shopping cart *prepopulated* to sign you up for two years of registration versus the one year you expected—and thus doubling the amount you pay—is disconcerting. Thrown into this unruly mix of sales tactics is an intermediary page that lists all related items you might want. Now, instead of making it obvious that all of this is optional, GoDaddy intentionally places the "No thanks, skip this and take me to the checkout" link at the bottom of this very long page in a tiny, nondescript font. The GoDaddy Web site seems set up to be deliberately confusing, and the result is that the first time a user enters, there's a good chance he or she will either abandon the effort or accidentally buy more than originally intended. Though the process seems to work for this company, I submit that this is not the best way forward for most online businesses.

While almost all Web sites will require users to set up accounts and log in to purchase, the very pinnacle of simplicity is to enable your checkout to process truly anonymous transactions. As anyone who has shopped online will tell you, it's a pain in the behind to set up and manage so many accounts. Seemingly every single Web site requires you to log in to make a purchase. It's the nature of the software, and it works very well with the marketing need to capture data on users for future use.

Some Web sites simplify this part of the process even further by using a third-party processing system. In doing so, you can enable shopping on your site while keeping the checkout procedure separate. To your users, the process appears seamlessly integrated, but, in fact, they leave your site to process the transaction. Such systems usually only require an e-mail address for verifying the transaction and for sending a receipt. The e-mails are not used for further marketing purposes. Other than needing to enter the required credit card billing information, there is no requirement to open an account.

While you may miss the opportunity to send e-mails to users at a later date by not making them register, such an approach can pay dividends via increased trust through seeming to be less intrusive. I was recently shopping online and came across such a system. I was faced with a page that asked if I wanted to open a full account or simply check out anonymously. The company gave explanations for each option, with the pros and cons clearly outlined. I chose the anonymous route, as I knew this would be a onetime purchase. Months later I still have not seen a single e-mail from the company—true to its word of not using the e-mail address I provided for marketing purposes. This goodwill, and the fact that the company kept its word through many ensuing holidays, very much attracts me to do business with the company again. It's a simple, informal contract, really: I requested that the company not hassle me, and it didn't. By holding up its end of this informal bargain, I'm very pleased with the company. Imagine that: do nothing and gain trust.

This part of the process is so important that I'm going to recommend another book here. Steve Krug's *Don't Make Me Think: A Common Sense Approach to Web Usability* should be required reading for anyone operating a Web site. In fact, ideally it should magically land on your bedside table when the first thought of starting a Web site filters through your brain; it's that important and useful.

■ ■ ■ Pillar of Trust 4: Follow-up

If you're going to have users log in when visiting, don't miss the opportunity to have registered users create wish lists. A wish list is a separate list where users can place items of interest without having to put them directly into a shopping cart. In this way, users accumulate items that they can purchase on their next visit. It's an excellent setup for a follow-up conversation with them after their initial visit.

A wish list is the perfect way to follow up with users to remind them they were interested in certain items. Many sites offer some form of this service, which is usually tied to a log in. When customers return, they are either taken directly to their wish lists as their first stop or a link is shown prominently to alert them to their lists.

By any measure, one of the top leaders in this area has to be eBay.com. If you ever have the desire to learn more about a complete selling experience, be sure to open up an eBay account, fill in all the details, and start watching items of interest. It doesn't matter if you never intend to purchase: by enabling the "Watch This Item" feature in your own account, you will set into motion one of the best user-engagement systems online today.

It's not surprising that it took a site with such a fast-moving service (auctions) to get this concept right. For every item watched, the clock is ticking. It might take hours, or even days, but at predetermined times prior to the auction's end, you will be notified via e-mail from eBay to check in on the item and note its progress. From my action of clicking the single "Watch This Item" link on the site, eBay is now reaching out to me multiple times to remind me I was interested and that the clock is ticking. My point here isn't to encourage you to start sending your visitors e-mails every day, but to urge you to seek ways to open the lines of communication. If a user takes the time to note on a wish list items he or she likes, you should make the effort to follow up to encourage completion of a sale.

If you are sensing a theme—that trust is important—you've gotten the message. Building trust with your users is critical in the online environment. Time and again it has been proven that building trust brings users back and increases brand retention, loyalty, word-of-mouth support, and revenues. Just as you know exactly where to shop in your local neighborhood, users online build their own three-dimensional map of an online community that works to support their needs. If you engender trust with your users, you will be included in their online community.

■ ■ ■ Pillar of Trust 5: Security

While users are researching the products they desire, they are close to making purchase decisions, but not quite ready yet. They're still looking for the clues they need to open their wallets. In fact, their wallets may be open and they're seeking to establish a trustworthy relationship. One in which they not only make a payment to you for a product or service, but place trust in you to protect their names, addresses, contact numbers, and credit card information. At this stage it is very important to make users feel at ease on your Web site. Given today's sophisticated checkout technology and the multilayered security built in via layers of encryption, there is very little reason for users to fear sharing their information.

As a Webmaster, you have the responsibility to ensure the existence and proper implementation of the layers of protection your visitors have come to expect. You may choose to seek discounted services and systems for other areas of your Web site, but for your shopping cart and its security, you should always try to implement the best you can afford. When the system is up and running, integrated and functioning as expected, don't miss the critical step of assuring users they are safe. Time is the ultimate indicator here, but during their first few interactions with you, it's important to remind visitors that they are indeed safe when transacting business via your Web site. You could take many routes to this end, such as these:

- Link to a page explaining in detail the encryption used and the safety protocols practiced.
- A logo provided from a vetting agency testifying to the level of safety acknowledged by the third-party company (see Figure 3.1).
- Testimonials from past customers testifying to the trust they have in your site. Note: While it might be tempting to simply invent these, don't. Users are savvy, and if the testimonials on your site don't match the general trend of conversation about your site elsewhere, such as in opinion-sharing sites like www.epinions.com, users will come to their own conclusions about your trustworthiness.

Figure 3.1. Logos testifying to the trustworthiness of the Web site

While it will require some effort to build trust and guide most users from search engines to making a purchase, a certain percentage are ready to purchase now. This latter group is fresh off their research trek and ready to lay down some money. They are quite savvy and feel they know exactly what they want. For visitors like this, exactly matching their expectations is critical.

For these users, the path through the Web site is clean and clear. They are at your Web site to make a purchase, so you need to ensure that nothing impedes this action. By having a very clear, clean, and logical navigational pathway through your site, users who already know what they want are able to find the exact product or service, place it in their carts, and check out quickly. For such users, any extras or add-ons that distract from the process of purchasing can be detrimental.

This is where the added attention to detail around structuring your Web site and pages will pay off. While all users will appreciate a greater number of large images and more detail about a product or service, taking care to arrange this information in a logical manner will help increase conversions. For users who know exactly what product or service they wish to purchase, however, any added steps in the process can be frustrating. This frustration is what leads to typically high abandonment rates of shopping carts. Users who know what they want to purchase wish only to have useful items shown to them, such as shipping calculators and delivery schedules. You should seize the opportunity to thoughtfully showcase related items, but take care that in doing so you do not distract users from their original intent to purchase.

One proven approach to optimizing your shopping cart and checkout process is to initially strip the entire process to the bare essentials. You will not be showing related products, shipping calculators, or any other useful add-ons in the process. By starting from this point, you can build and track, through conversion data, exactly which enhancements would prove beneficial or detrimental. It might turn out that users respond much better to information about shipping than to information about related products. At that point you would know you should incorporate and highlight shipping information on the page.

In order to accurately gauge what each change brings to the equation, be sure to limit your testing to one change at a time. In this manner, you will be able to construct a very clear view of the elements that have positive and negative impacts on your conversions. This information will also act as a proxy to help you understand how your users are interacting with your Web site. If adding shipping and delivery information increases conversions, this will be borne out in your metrics. By moving forward one step at a time, you can clearly understand which elements will add value to the conversion process for your users and drive revenues up for yourself, and which items are blockers and turn users off.

It is clear that developing trust is a driving force in converting traffic from organic search marketing. Sure, your Web site should be well designed and the checkout process streamlined, but users researching a purchase still need to be coaxed along the path toward the point of parting with their money, and engendering the feeling of trust is pivotal to making that happen.

As you'll see in the next chapter, users who come to your site through paid search marketing are much closer to the purchase decision already, so you can and should handle them differently. Your ability to track data on them is much deeper, given the systems employed, so you'll be making decisions based on hard numbers with this crowd. Paid search can be a conversion hunter's best friend.

4

Paid Search Marketing: Driving Customers to Your Web Site

■ ■ ■　How to Get Started

By now everyone should be familiar with the concept of paid search. These are the ads that appear at the top and along the right-hand side of a Web page when you make a query on a search engine. Paid search remains the easiest and fastest way to develop traffic at any of the three major search engines. Each program differs slightly, but in broad terms they share many similarities. Whether it's through Google, Yahoo, or Bing, these programs tend to run basically the same. Not to imply that these systems run in *exactly* the same way, though—far from it. Each of the systems is unique, and each has nuances of its own.

Generally speaking, the main function of using paid search with an engine revolves around your paying for ad placement. Like an auction, you bid on a term to show your ad in a paid system. The rule of thumb is that the higher your bid, the higher your ad placement is on the page at the search engine. Each bid is tied to a single keyword or phrase, so think carefully when planning your budget, as this can get expensive. Coupled with your bids is an intelligence layer that understands how your advertisements and landing pages actually perform and convert.

All of this data, when combined, provides the search engine with a detailed overview of your Web site's performance. This data is readily available to you through the reporting interface in your account at each engine, and you should become familiar with it and use it to help make decisions on how to place future bids, how to edit and modify your ads, and which landing pages to tweak. In fact, this information is so critical that in some cases landing pages may be rejected because the search engines know they will not perform well.

Google in particular goes to great lengths to ensure that Webmasters have detailed tools and systems to help optimize their paid search campaigns. By using Google's Web site optimizer, tracking information and testing options available through AdWords, you now have the impressive ability to fine-tune a paid ad campaign yourself. Google truly does make it easy to spend your money. With its wealth of knowledge from years of experience in watching these campaigns unfold, Google's search engines are in a unique position to help guide you to success. After all, guiding you to success makes Google more successful.

It is important to have a plan when you enter into paid search. With keywords today costing upwards of $5, $10, or even $20 per click, your expenses can mount quickly when running paid search campaigns at the major engines. Each search engine charges differently for each keyword or phrase, so keeping an eye on your total expenditure when managing paid search campaigns will require work on your part. For many popular terms the days of low-cost volume traffic are behind us. If your focus is in each area, however, you can still find a lot of value. While no system allows bids at one penny these days, a lot of traffic can be had at $.10 per click. Your goal is to ensure that from your advertisement for your landing page all your efforts are optimized toward generating a conversion. The engines will work hand in hand with you to ensure that your goals are met.

While it is impossible to review each system in detail as it stands today, I can tell you from personal experience that the systems run by the three major search engines can be used to generate a lot of traffic and a lot of conversions when optimized properly. Properly optimizing your landing pages, and the advertisements themselves, is relatively straightforward. As mentioned before, the engines have tools to help you understand which decisions to make and how to modify your pages and ads to improve performance. Some people might overlook these tools, thinking they are only designed to increase the search engines' profits. Naturally, the search engines seek to increase profits, however, they also see you as a willing ally in this effort. Therefore, their goal is to arm you with the right information to be successful and to reach your own goals. This is a case of win-win for both parties.

■ ■ ■ How to Optimize Your Ads and Your Landing Page

You should be methodical when you begin your first search campaign. Each of the engines has dedicated training, which you should take from beginning to end to fully understand the systems before you start spending your hard-earned money on paid advertising campaigns designed to drive traffic to your Web site. It is easy to burn through thousands of dollars in a few days, see a sharp increase in traffic, yet still have no conversions to show for it. By following the engine's guidance and best practices, simple as they may seem, you set a solid baseline from which to start. The tools of the engine will walk you through everything from well-thought-out and well-designed advertisements to improvements you can make on your landing pages to increase conversions.

This last part is critical. It is often the small details that make the difference when improving a Web page for conversions by using the tracking tools available through the platforms of the engines. You can clearly see where users abandoned your site during the purchase process, and this information will help you to pinpoint your weaknesses. While you can use paid search strictly to drive traffic, this is usually not recommended. This can be an incredibly expensive way to drive traffic in an effort to increase page views and ad click-through rates. Far better for your efforts to drive traffic is to use organic search marketing (SEO). Paid search excels at driving to your Web site clients who are ready to convert.

As with everything in search engine marketing, keyword research is a critical step. The engines will help guide you through this information clearly in their systems. Paid search platforms are unique in that they have a history of understanding which keywords have converted successfully across the entire ecosystem of Web sites involved in running paid ads. While you will not get direct knowledge of which words worked on which Web sites, the collective intelligence that's accessible will help you very quickly hone in on what works for you. Therefore, one of your main goals should be to do your keyword research early—it's the starting point for any successful paid search campaign.

Following this, you will need to actually write the advertisements that will displayed on a user's search engine results page (SERP). These ads have limitations placed on them by the engines, so reading through the documentation and how-to guides is important and will save you time in setting up your ads. Be sure to prominently display the keywords you are targeting. This measure has proven to increase click rates and deliver users to Web sites. On the search engine, the exact matching is indicated with bold text in the ad itself. As in the organic rankings, this designation is to alert the user to an exact match for the phrase that was searched. Do not miss the opportunity to put that keyword at the very beginning of your ad whenever possible.

While the systems can help you understand how to write a compelling ad that will elicit a click response, ensuring that those users will actually convert when they land on your Web site is mostly up to you. Knowing that different Web sites will achieve different levels of success, the engines have stepped in and will help you understand how to optimize your efforts by offering direct advice on making edits to your ads and landing pages to improve results. This information resides inside your paid search account.

A Unique Landing Page

A landing page is any page a user is sent to upon clicking on an ad. These pages usually are dedicated specifically to the information in the ad a user clicks on. In many cases, however, they can be actual pages that currently exist on your Web site. There is no official rule that says a landing page must be one or the other. There is, however, a great deal of study put into the success of conversions on dedicated landing pages, and given their high success rate, it's not surprising that most people choose to run unique landing pages with their paid search campaigns. To be clear, you can use any page on your Web site as the location where a paid search ad directs traffic, but using a unique landing page is usually the way to go.

Such unique pages exist to serve one purpose only: to get users to buy the product or service you mentioned in the ad they just clicked, so the pages should be designed to speak only of the actual product. These pages are not ones you'd link to in your normal Web site navigation, though, as they are simply a means of converting sales and make sense only when viewed immediately after the paid search ad is clicked. Otherwise, they might seem a bit abrupt or random.

Running a unique landing page to directly match a search campaign gives you the added ability to craft a completely customized sales message for each keyword or group of key words an advertisement targets. In this way you present the user with a very clear and clean pathway to the conversion. If the pages on your Web site are designed in such a way that they contain only the relevant and needed information on a given product or service, then they may well be candidates to serve as landing pages for paid campaigns. Take this thinking one step further and make sure that the data and information shown on these pages drive users into the sales funnel and through to the conversion.

Often, a dedicated landing page is a much simpler version of the standard Web page. Through the systems available at search engines and their platforms, you can run a number of tests with an infinite variety of subtle changes on the page. All this testing is designed to help you understand which version of a page converts the best. The results may differ between products, services, search engines, and keywords. The point here is to use the tools and the information to help you finely tune each landing page to a specific keyword or set of keywords. If this sounds like a lot of work, it usually is. Your best bet is to start small and grow as your experience and revenues increase. Taking this approach will save you a lot of time and headache as you progress toward more expensive keywords. Getting things wrong with a short list of key words and a handful of landing pages is easily managed; getting things wrong with 10,000 keywords and hundreds of landing pages is extremely costly.

Be sure to set up individual campaigns within the search engines' paid advertising systems to better track your results and efforts. These systems are incredibly detailed, and you should use that to your advantage. By setting up individual campaigns, which are then mapped to select advertisements targeting select keywords or phrases, you can quickly drill down to see which areas are performing well and which are lagging behind. This data, coupled with the systems scanning your landing pages, will help you understand where you are losing people in the conversion process, and give you a true picture of where to apply your efforts. This data paints a clear image of exactly how users are interacting with your Web site. You will likely learn that users originating from a paid search will click through fewer pages than those who originate from an organic search. Your goal at this point is to try to fix the conversion process to capture those users and ensure they end up on your well-designed landing pages.

Example of Providing Information to Convert a User

Let's look at an example of how to get this conversion process correct with a dedicated landing page (Figure 4.1). The search query used was *Jeep Wrangler speakers*. The actual search engine results page at Google looked like this, and we're

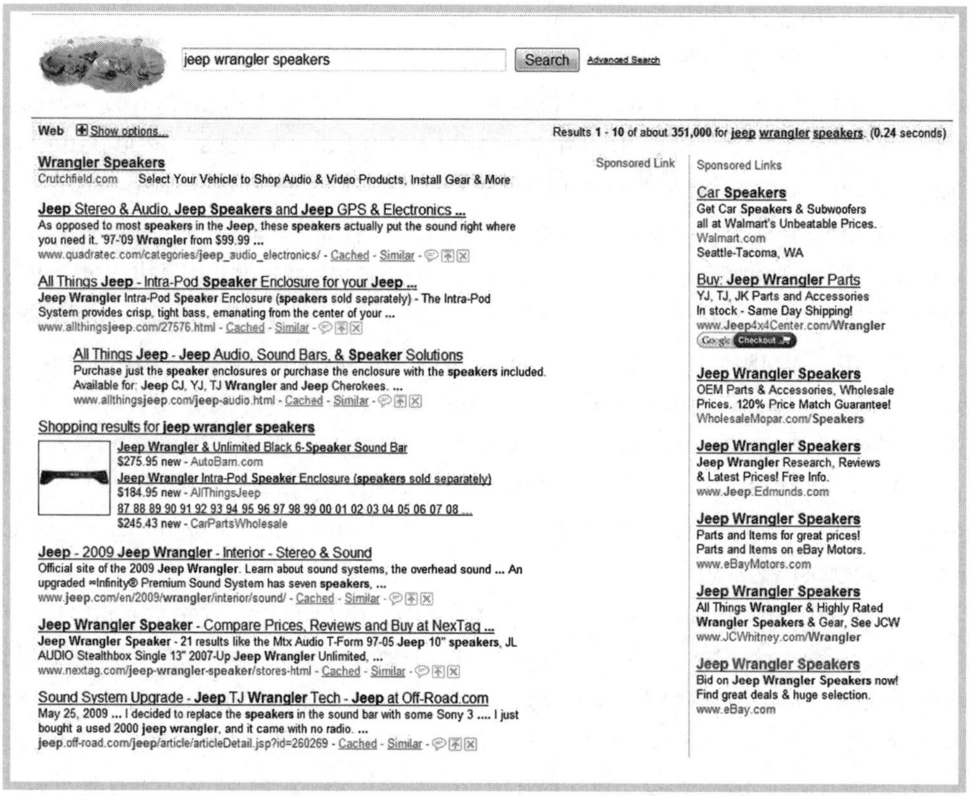

Figure 4.1. Paid search ads for Jeep Wrangler speakers

seeing the JCWhitney.com ad, second from the bottom on the right-hand side of the image:

They are not bidding as competitively on this ad as others are, therefore their ad shows lower on the page. Another reason the ad may be showing lower is the actual results the advertiser has seen with this particular ad. The search engine tracks the click activity on each ad and factors that into determining the order in which the ads appear. Ensuring that an ad is well crafted can help the ad rank higher in the queue simply because a well-written, compelling ad generates more user interaction; in this case, it generates more clicks. The results and conversion rates for JCWhitney's competitors must be lower than those of the selected advertiser, shown here. When users click on all of the ads prior to JCWhitney.com's, they are taken to generic landing pages, which require further information and action on the part of users before they can get to the information they originally searched for. This will frustrate some buyers and cause them to leave the Web site.

In the example, you see that JC Whitney gets it right. This advertiser is targeting a dedicated phrase, using it properly in its paid ad, and when users click on the ad, they are delivered directly to a page specific to what they were looking for. The ad itself is a direct match to the query entered. Within the ad, two of the main keywords are highlighted. Clicking on them will bring you to the landing in Figure 4.2.

The landing page itself is a model of direct action and clear information. Users immediately understand that what they were searching for is being presented to them. Instead of having to look through the Web site to find the content they were after, they can take an action to view the information and products they initially wanted. Since the initial query—while targeted to a specific make and model of speaker—was vague in the actual product itself, the landing page allows for a variety of options. From here, users can quickly narrow down their needs by selecting from one of six main options. The page is clean and clear and makes it obvious to the user in which direction to proceed. This is an excellent example of a clean landing page doing a good job of providing information that will help convert users. When they come to this page, the navigational information, additional categories, and further advertising information is clearly laid out, but does not detract from the goal of showing users the exact content they requested.

Figure 4.2. Landing page for Jeep Wrangle speakers

■ ■ ■ How to Get a Conversion

Converting users from paid search is about simplifying the path through the sales process. While the goal of your landing page is to ensure that users see the correct information when they land on your Web site, from here your systems must be properly aligned to make sure they keep users on the right path to making the purchase. An overly complicated checkout process can kill even the most successful of paid search campaigns. By shortening and streamlining your transaction process, you encourage users to complete the purchase.

Search engines will gladly provide tracking for you, which you can integrate into your confirmation of sale Web page to understand whether each user has completed the process. Further, the paid search platform itself is then capable of generating an ROI (return on investment) figure for you, if you enable it by installing the tracking code the search engine gives you on your confirmation page (the page that shows completed purchases and that thanks users for their business). This step is critical in understanding whether you're progressing in the right direction. While it is true that users interacting with paid search are much further along the sales funnel than users with organic listings, it is important to speed users through the conversion process to ensure that you don't simply lose them.

As you can see, paid search is a much straighter path to conversions. It's important to remember to watch your ROI and decide up front if the costs will be manageable. Some clicks today cost upward of $10 each (that's where those huge profits for search engines come from, you know—expensive ad revenues). You'd better make sure your landing pages, sales messages, and checkout process are super-refined before you start paying that kind of money to drive traffic to your Web site.

Another area of search marketing that is very popular today is "local search." As the name implies, this affords a business the opportunity to be found relative to its geographic location. Odd as it might sound, conducting a local search requires that you have a physical address and a phone number, but not a Web site. This is one area where the lines of search marketing blur a bit, revealing a hidden opportunity for businesses with bricks and mortar to back them up. We'll discuss this in more detail in the next chapter.

5

Local Search Marketing: Narrowing Your Scope

How to Get Started

When we speak of actual local search, we are referring to the ability to locate and find specific businesses in specific locations. An example of this would be a locksmith ranking well for a search on locksmith services in a select city or community. This mode of search works particularly well for local businesses. If you are primarily online, or have no local storefront, the concepts discussed around "localization" in this chapter will still be of interest, but true local search requires an address and phone number in a location.

There are two components you must understand in order to be successful in local search. The first is the concept of localization, and then the idea of local search itself. When Web sites speak of local search, they often refer to being found in a specific location or across multiple specific locations. For example, you may want your Web site to be found for a particular product in all areas that are most likely to consume this product. If your product is ski wax, it would make sense to appear in search results originating from any area that enjoys an active skiing culture. While this may seem like a great idea, local search is not without its challenges. In localization, you

51

are trying to be associated with many regions, but you may not necessarily have a physical location in any of them.

Let's take a look at two examples that will clarify the differences between localization and local search. In this first example (Figure 5.1), the results brought back from the Bing decision engine are localized. If you look down through the results, you'll see that each of the top 10 items shown will deliver the goods. In this case, said goods are details about the weather in San Diego, California.

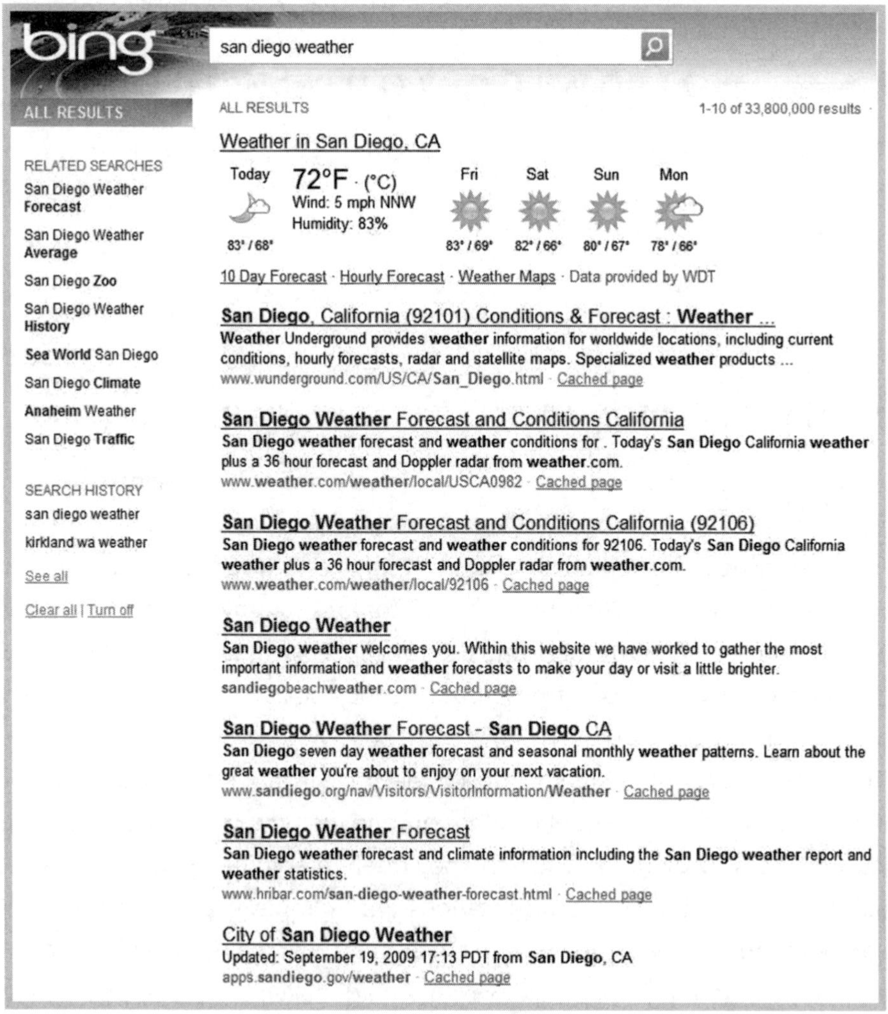

Figure 5.1. Bing local search results

This is not, however, a local search. Weather.com and wunderground.com are not local businesses in these areas. Even if they do have a physical location in a specific area, their goal is to show information broadly across a wide spectrum of areas; globally, in fact. This is an example of localized search. Now let's contrast that example with a true local search and see the differences.

In this example (Figure 5.2), we see what a true local search brings back. Most obvious is the map populated with a number of items, which you can click on and zoom in to see in more detail.

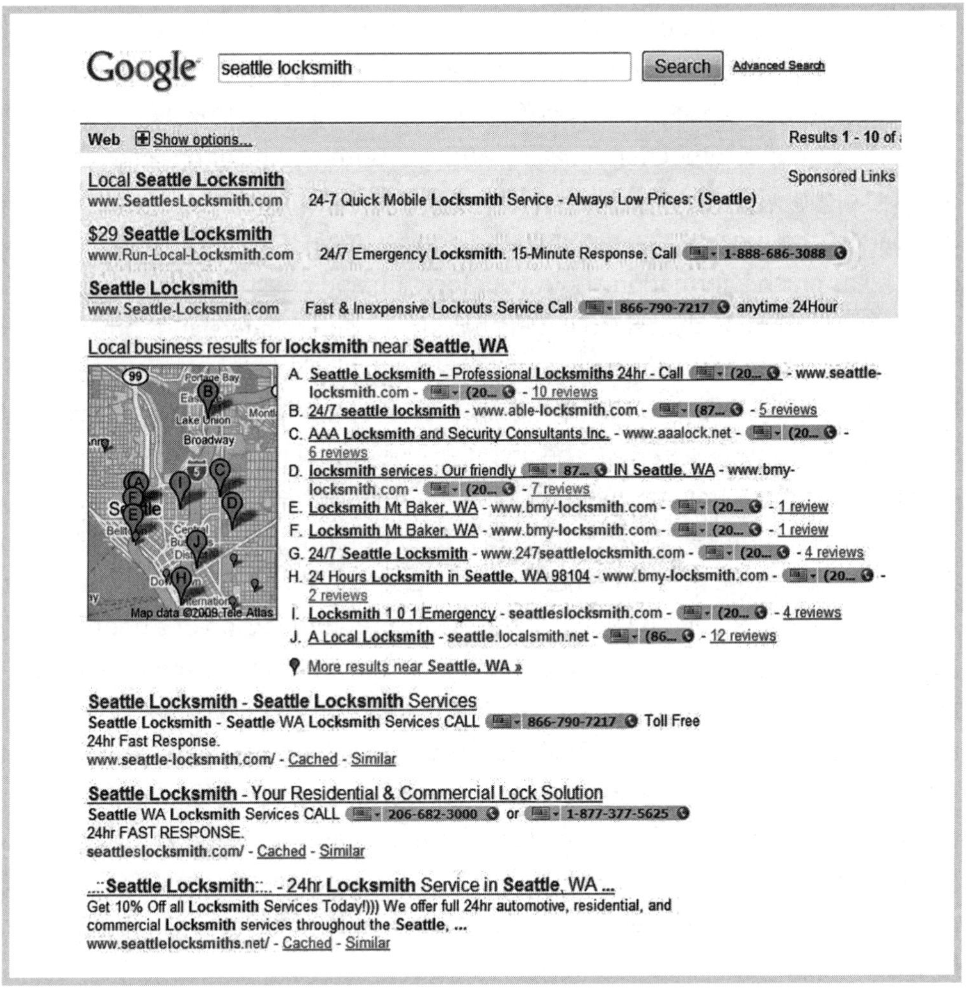

Figure 5.2. Google local search results

Obvious in the local search results are phone numbers and addresses. The rest of the results on the search page, whether paid or organic, are a mix of local businesses as well. One main differentiator between localized search and local search is the need for a Web site. Businesses can be found quickly and easily through local search with the most pertinent information on hand: a phone number and physical address. There is no need to have an actual Web site to participate in local search. This might seem counterintuitive, but when you understand that searchers are actually looking for a specific service in most local searches, it becomes clear that what they need are directions to a product or service and a contact number so they can find out if this product or service is available immediately.

In local search, you will enter into a process with a search engine to identify yourself and associate yourself with a specific area and location. You'll be required to provide a local phone number and mailing address, both of which the search engine can opt to contact with confirmation information for you. When you've completed that part of the process, you can help the engine understand more about you by entering as much information about your location and area of service as possible. The more information the search engine has, the better it understands how to rank your Web site in a search engine results page like the list you see above.

Here's a quick run-through of the process of signing up a business for local search with Google (Figure 5.3). The first step involves filling in the blanks to come up with the information shown in the "ad" on the right-hand side of this page.

The information contained in this ad is fictitious, but you will note there is no Web site listed in the ad. None is needed to appear in the local search results. It's similar to being in the phone book, or the search engine's version of a phone book. No actual Web site is needed, as they show your name, location, and phone number when users in your area search for your services or products. Google uses the information you provide on the first page, as well as all the information on this and subsequent pages, to understand exactly what your business is about. Don't take shortcuts. Make sure you fill in as much information as possible so that the search engine can rank you as a relevant result. If this means going outside and taking photographs of your business, products, or services in action, then you should do it and upload the photos into your profile.

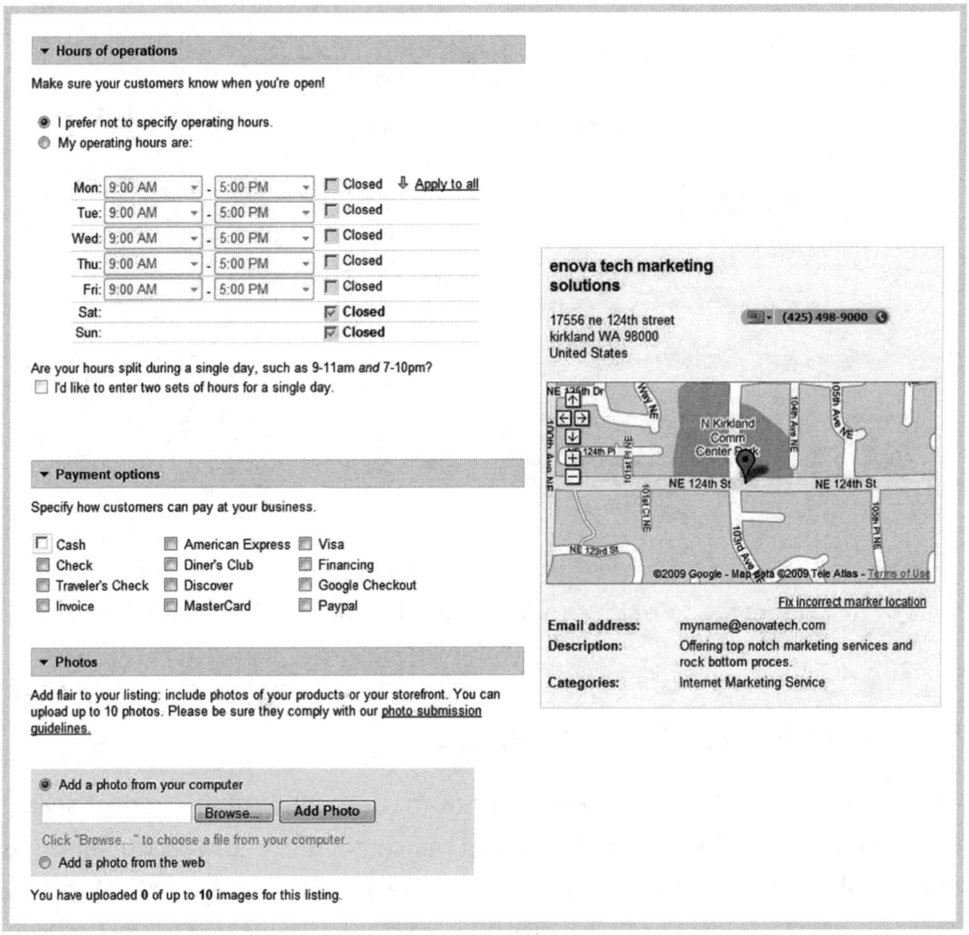

Figure 5.3. Signing up a business for a local search

In this next screen shot (Figure 5.4), you can see the options available to you for verifying your ad. A technician at the search engine will contact you by phone or will mail to the address you provided a postcard containing a confirmation number. Once you get this number, you can then go back to your account and verify it, after which your ad will be placed live.

If you look at the differences between the ads in the first and second images, you will notice that I added payment types to further help my (fictitious) users understand about my services and options with my (fictitious) business.

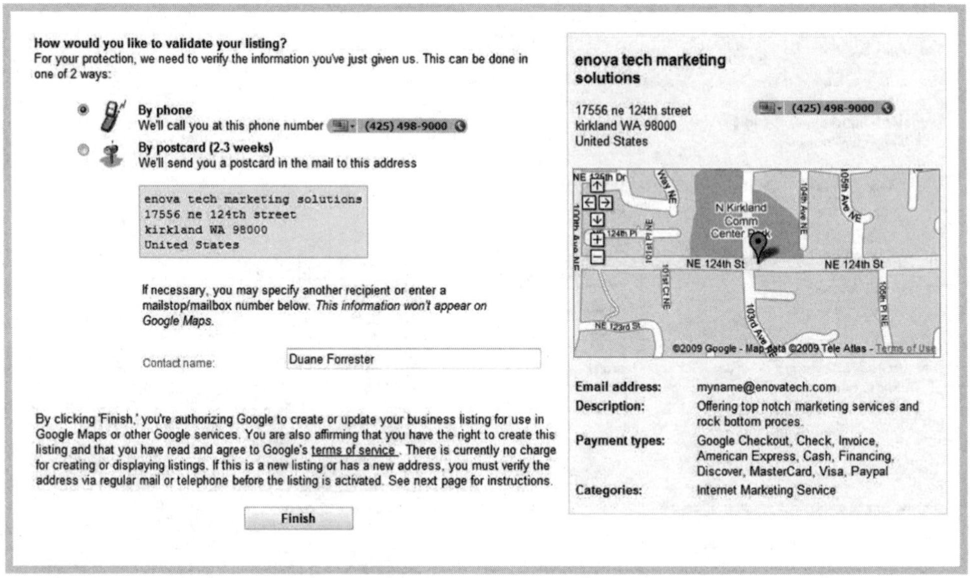

Figure 5.4. Verifying your ad for a local search

Converting through local channels varies from converting other forms of search marketing. If we're talking about localized search, then the conversion pattern is quite similar. For true local search where you are a business in a specific location, converting traffic from your ad will take cues from old-school business tactics. How you treat your customers will determine if they come back to you or seek another service in the future. How quickly you return a phone call or e-mail can make all the difference between gaining a new client or missing an opportunity.

With local search, it is critical to remember that users are looking for something in their immediate vicinity right now. If you are a plumber and someone is searching for a plumber, you should be prepared to respond to an emergency call. Different categories will have different means of response. People generally don't phone a plumber unless they're in dire need of help. In many cases businesses such as these will have a 24-hour hotline that users can phone. So you need to ensure that if you have such a number, it's listed in your local ad. Furthermore, if you have an e-mail address shown in your ad, it may be wise to use a smart phone to enable users to e-mail you directly and reach you immediately. Again, it is critical to the conversion of these customers that you respond quickly when they reach out to you. True local search is about getting your telephone to ring or delivering traffic through your front door. It is always prudent to remember that it's much harder to gain new clients than to keep current clients happy.

Now, while local search may be pushing the boundaries of what Web search is, our next chapter drills down on one of the newest forms of online marketing. Videos and Webinars are among the hottest ways to attract attention and cement your position as a topic authority. Relatively inexpensive, both of these great options leave you with plenty of room to show your style, impress with your knowledge, and leave visitors feeling that you offer quality products and services.

6

Videos and Webinars: Profit from Sharing Your Knowledge

BY USING VIDEO to interact with your users, you can create a rich experience that they will appreciate. You can use this appreciation to establish a solid relationship with them, which will generate repeat visits to acquire the newest updates.

Interacting through videos and Webinars can help build credibility in your users' eyes. And as you've read elsewhere in this book, boosting credibility also has an effect on boosting conversions. By leveraging users' attention on your video, you can place a subtle message and your brand clearly within their field of vision for an extended period of time. There is ample space in today's video world to include things such as your logo, a tagline, and your domain. Keep in mind that you can edit the video as you see fit and add a small header or footer area to contain this information.

How to Get Started

With the advent and proliferation of video online, video search has become more prevalent over the past few years. Video sites such as YouTube and Google video made mainstream consumption of video online an everyday occurrence. It did not take long for businesses to understand that video was an ideal medium for communicating with potential customers.

A video search today will turn up videos for almost any topic. It is important to remember, though, that while major search engines such as Bing and Google may show video results, they still have a hard time understanding what the actual content of a given video is. This is because search engines do not consume video in the same manner as humans do. Search engine and video platforms cannot process images visually nor can they understand context. Humans *see* video; platforms *show* video. These engines and platforms therefore rely on video creators' or users' content tags, related keywords, and transcription information from the video.

When all of the above-mentioned cues are incorporated, a search engine will have a clear understanding of what a given video is about. Yet many videos today are simply uploaded with no contextual information provided. This leads to inaccurate search results when you ask YouTube or Google video to bring back footage on a topic. It is a big challenge for the search engines to match not only your intended query, but to return content that is relevant, accurate, and rich. Often, a search engine may not be aware that video content applicable to a query exists, due to a lack of tagging or contextual information.

When you provide a video to a source such as Google video, you should take the time to fill in all the blanks to ensure that the engine understands what your video is about. By doing so, you not only provide the queues that the search engine needs to rank your video well, but you also provide important information to help users decide whether they should click on your video or another in the list. If you post videos regularly, this process will quickly become familiar to you. Posting with the relevant contextual information requested on your upload page should not be overlooked—it is the first step, and probably the most important one, to ensuring that your video is properly optimized.

Let's go into some video optimization best practices to get your videos ranking well in the search results. See Appendix 1 for a list of Web sites to which you can submit your videos in order to increase your exposure.

■ ■ ■　Create Unique, Useful Videos

Nothing is worse than performing a video search and finding a hundred useless results. Normally when performing a video search, you have a specific item in mind. You start with a keyword or a key phrase and look for related video content. When you click the "Submit Query" button and see a list that is very deep yet populated with videos of short duration and no contextual information, you're left disappointed and frustrated. So, when creating a video, make it useful and unique. I know—easier said than done—but unique, useful content is a good way to help you stand out in a sea of pointless, time-wasting videos.

This does not mean you have to rack your brain for new ideas that haven't been explored. You can make a perfectly unique and useful video commenting on something already newsworthy by developing your own voice and articulating your own opinions on the topics of the day. In other words, create your personal take on a topic by fashioning a video based upon your point of view. The topic might not be new, but your viewpoint will be.

Elsewhere in this book we cover ways of developing "hooks" to develop user interaction, and these hooks can also be used to draw attention when you create your video. With a little practice, you can become proficient in sharing your own perspective on a wide variety of subjects.

Keep Videos Short

The most effective videos are short—around three minutes. Longer videos occupy more storage space, take longer to upload, and, depending on the Internet connection employed, can take much longer to download. If your goal is to captivate and convert viewers, you want the process on their end to be as quick and painless as possible. Going longer than three minutes is fine—as is going shorter—but keep in mind that while you may be creating excellent content, if it takes too long to load, users will simply click on the next video in the search list. Getting the length just right will take some practice. It's likely that the first few times you produce a video, it will go much longer than three minutes. Again, with practice it will become second nature to you, and you'll be producing useful videos in no time.

One area in which you can extend the length of time for your video is product reviews. Users are generally more willing to wait for this type of video to load, because they're looking specifically for information on the product they searched for. This means you can run videos much longer than three minutes in these situations, still capture the users' attention, and have a lot more exposure for your domain name and brand. After all, users will have expressed an interest in a specific product or service. And as they interact more frequently with your reviews to build trust with you, they'll come to see you as an authority on the topic.

Contextual Guidance

As stated above, a search engine cannot actually see the video content as people do, so it is important to provide guidance about the subject matter of the video. You can do this by embedding your video on a page and wrapping content related to the topic around the video itself. The search engines will register this as a cue that the embedded video is related to the content surrounding it.

An excellent way to enable this contextual guidance and ensure a great user experience is to provide a written transcript of the content of the video itself. When you create your video, include either a bullet point list or short script. This information can then be reused as the text or transcript to place near the video when you upload it into your online video hosting account. YouTube.com is the obvious Web site for sharing videos, and there is space in a YouTube account to input that text so that it appears near the actual video when displayed online. You can use this same approach if you host your own videos on your Web site. Insert the video into the page and place the text next to it on the page. Since users will see this information on the page itself or near the video on a video search service, make sure that the content is grammatically correct and legible.

- **Title.** Optimizing your title for a video is very important. Inserting keywords you are targeting—those related to the topic of the video, for example—into your title, and keeping your title to around 65 characters will help optimize it. This is the first clue for the search engines to understand the topic and relevance of a video. Be certain to include your most relevant keyword or phrase in your title and keep information as tightly related to the video content or topic as possible.

- **Tags.** Tagging your video ensures that relevant related keywords are associated with the content. The best way to capture related search traffic is to use phrases that, while not as popular as those used in your title tag, are strongly associated with the content.
- **Keyword "video."** When searching for a particular video, many people actually use the word "video" in their search query. It is therefore a good practice to work the word "video" into your title and your tags. By doing so, you give the search engines a clue that this is video content related to a specific keyword or phrase, with the result that they come closer to returning an exact match for the user search query.
- **Targeted key phrases.** Be sure to target specific areas into which to work your key phrases. Using targeted key phrases emphasizes the relevance and focus of the video content on a specific topic. A great opportunity here is to work a specific phrase or keyword into the file name for the video itself. As you'll see in the next step, you can take this even further.

Optimize URLs

Optimized URLs are short and keyword-rich, and search engines love them. By optimizing your URLs you will be able to place related relevant keywords into folder and file names. This helps guide search engines toward understanding the relevance of your video content regarding a specific topic. Again, it is critical that the search engines understand what your videos are about, as they cannot actually view the content themselves.

- **Video site maps.** Much in the way that a site map outlines the content of your Web site and makes it accessible for a search engine, you should follow the same best practices to produce your video site maps. Keep dedicated site maps and update them whenever you produce a new video. This will help the search engines index your content quickly.
- **Inbound linking.** When you share your videos, always link back to them using the keywords with which you want the video to be identified in the anchor text of the link. To clarify, this is the actual text that is linked; it is the text users would click on to get to your video. By including

relevant keywords or phrases in this anchor text, you give the search engines a clue about the content they are about to see. As these links pass value from one Web site to another, that value is accrued against the actual page. Inbound links to your content and videos are like "votes" from other Web sites. Given time and enough links, your content will be deemed valuable enough to rank very well in search results.

- **Upload to video sharing sites.** Hosting videos on your own Web site is one thing, but uploading them to video sharing sites can be the key to finding thousands of viewers every day. These sites have targeted audiences globally, and thus are an excellent way to reach a specific group of people in whom you're interested. See Appendix 1 for a list of video upload sites, courtesy of www.reelseo.com.
- **Allow "embed code."** Be certain to enable "embed code," which will allow users to share your video with others. While it may take a little bit of work if you're hosting your own videos, Web sites such as YouTube make this process simple by providing the links and information you need. By enabling this functionality, you encourage users to share your video on their own Web sites and blogs, which can dramatically increase the reach of your video product. And while enabling the embed functionality, you still retain credit and ownership of content, while permitting viral sharing.

User-Generated Content

While sometimes difficult to police, user-generated content is often worth the added value, especially around video content. You should encourage users to leave comments about what they have seen. Not only will such comments move other users to watch your content, but they will help contextually fill in information about the video for a search engine. More total comments from users can increase your page depth and overall relevance. Just be sure to keep a close eye on the comments to make certain that "spammers" aren't trying to drop links from your Web site to theirs. Policing this area of your site will require time and effort, but some content management systems, such as the Wordpress platform, have widgets that can help. Don't let potential spam issues turn you off to this idea, as it can be very rewarding not only to see the comments pile up on your content but also to reap the rewards of conversations generated in the community that can prove invaluable down the road for your Web site to rank well overall.

- **Syndication.** Enabling a simple RSS or MRSS (media RSS) feed will allow you to syndicate your content so others may use it. RSS, which stands for either Rich Site Summary or Really Simple Syndication, depending upon whom you ask, is a powerful tool to aid in the distribution of your video content. In fact, if you publish content frequently, you may wish to enable an MRSS feed, as sites such as Google video prefer this format for ingesting your content. By enabling such a feed, the moment you publish your video, it's sent directly to Google for inclusion in its index.
- **Thumbnails.** Whenever you see a video surfacing on a search engine, there is a snapshot or thumbnail from that video. The point behind the thumbnail is to try to give users some form of context to understand what the video is about. Sites such as YouTube allow users to select different areas in your video from which to pull the thumbnail to see if it is visually appealing.

■ ■ ■ How to Get Conversions

Video is a great way to interact with your users, but they won't come to your site for just any video. You must take the time to make as professional a video as possible, as this effort will reflect on your services and Web site. Making a good impression with users who are viewing your video will encourage them to visit your Web site. A very effective video format to drive users to your site is product or service reviews, so we will concentrate on these in this section. People shopping online today often seek reviews of products or services prior to making a purchase. It helps them make an informed decision. You help encourage users to seriously consider the purchase by not only explaining the product, but by allowing them to see someone interact with it. While large glossy images are great for showing off products, users enjoy an added dimension when watching someone interact with a specific product via a video.

As a quick tip, you can produce videos inexpensively using a normal point-and-shoot camera with video capability. Some of today's cameras offer high-definition video capture as well. But video serving Web sites are not quite ready for full HD capabilities. Just make sure the background is uncluttered and that your camera is steady. It may require a few takes to get things just right, but the time will be worth it. Your instincts and actions will become honed over time, and you will be able to produce videos more quickly.

If you're embedding video on your own Web page, take time to make sure the products or service offerings are shown very close to the video window, allowing users to notice these items. If you're using a service such as YouTube, set up a dedicated account and fully populate all of the profile information offered to you. Users will see your domain and logo and link directly to your Web site. Video sharing Web sites also take care to ensure that users can easily share links to your video socially or embed your video directly on their own Web sites or blogs. All of these links lead directly back to the video you have uploaded through your account, again offering added exposure for your logo, your domain, and links to your products and services.

As you can see in Figure 6.1, Kelley Blue Book posted a review of the Toyota Prius on YouTube. The very beginning of this video prominently showcases for users the company's logo, name, and domain. This helps build brand awareness and instills confidence that the Web site can be trusted. In addition, it is worth noting that the actual title of the video also bears the name of the company. To the right of the page in the image is a "Subscribe" button. By subscribing, you easily access more related content from this provider, as well as direct links to information on its own Web site. This is an excellent way to drive users from the video product on YouTube to a Web site, which is why so many businesses do it. By using the YouTube platform, you enable users to quickly share this information with others. This video has been viewed almost 7,000 times to date. All that exposure drives traffic directly to the company's Web site.

The close-up of the lower portion of the video screen (Figure 6.2) shows what users watching the actual video would see. The bar with the Web site name along the bottom of the screen remains in place for the entire video session. This is an excellent location to overlay text information related to the video, for even though such information would not be visible to search engines, its inclusion does improve the user experience, as well as provide an excellent place for a company logo or tagline.

Figure 6.1. YouTube

If you're producing video content on a frequent basis, you can also take the step of inserting special, limited-time offers into your videos. This tactic works well to encourage users to take action with your Web site to complete a transaction. It should be noted, however, that you need a relatively high number of viewers consuming your video product in order for it to pay off. Not everyone who sees the message will take action, so the more people viewing your video, the more success you will enjoy.

Figure 6.2. YouTube close-up

■ ■ ■ Webinars

A Webinar is an excellent way to generate leads, influence purchase decisions, and build your place as a leader in your field. You may be tempted to view a Webinar as a video pitch, but that's not necessarily the case. Far from something you place on YouTube for people to find, a Webinar is a way to connect directly with people looking for your products or services in a timely, educational, and influential way. A well-run Webinar generates a lot of press and many inbound links, and also provides a direct path to converting prequalified leads. In addition, a Webinar can populate your lead generation pipeline with solid prospects.

It takes a bit of time, and some experimentation, to find the right formula for your Webinar needs, but it's well worth exploring. For those who are camera shy, a Webinar can be an excellent vehicle for exposure, since usually you are displaying a slide show as opposed to addressing a crowd directly. Having said this, you might not always want to be the face/voice behind your Webinar. We'll go into this later.

A Webinar is an excellent way to generate:

1. Education
2. Expertise
3. Leads

While many believe that a Webinar is simply a form of video advertising, there's a lot more going on in your typical Webinar than in your average marketing video. Add to this the fact that those participating in a Webinar see them as educational, and you have an ideal path to generating conversions. A Webinar is viewed as a professional learning experience presented by a company. It is implied that the job of a Webinar is to "sell" products or services, though the most successful ones generally avoid direct calls to "purchase." Then how can they convert, you ask?

Influence. That's how.

Users who sign up to take a Webinar are prequalified as interested in a topic. That's one big hurdle already overcome. During the sign-up process, you've also captured their e-mail addresses, so hurdle two (establishing a basis for communication) is also overcome. Now, before you go sending them a sales-oriented e-mail, it's best to remember that a Webinar is a subtle form of selling. Putting the cart before the horse by sending a sales message after users register but before they see the Webinar is a classic way to fail. So your primary focus is on making sure you give users value before asking them to purchase something. Your secondary focus is on resisting the temptation to send them sales e-mails just because you now can reach them that way.

Your goal with a Webinar is to expose users to your products, services, or way of thinking in a subtle, no-sales manner. You should be thinking, "How can I entice users to do business with me without directly asking for the sale?" The answer is to arm users with enough facts and confidence so that their decision to do business with you is easy and obvious. They main point here is that even as you are influencing users, they feel they are making the decision on their own, and you are the best choice.

By sharing your expertise on the topic, users end up informed and influenced. Part of the reason they paid attention to the Webinar is because they wanted to learn more about the topic. Whether you were known to them before this engagement doesn't matter. When the Webinar ends, they will know you are an expert.

Now, before we go too far down the path here, allow me to clarify something: you should not be hosting the Webinar. Yes, it makes sense for you to do the talking during portions that are highly detailed or technical, but given that a Webinar is not meant to become a technical briefing, your involvement should be limited. Instead, you should look to other experts or thought leaders on the topic to present the Webinar on your behalf. This creates a buffer between you, the business, and the end users. This buffer creates comfort in users, as they feel even less sales pressure. Consider using a third-party expert presenter as a living, breathing testimonial to your viewers. Their excitement and experience will provide all the "sell" message needed.

The thoughts expressed by a third party are often viewed as more believable by users as well. By bringing in a "ringer" to present the information on your behalf, you build a level of credibility that you might not earn by presenting yourself. Feel free to do the intros, but have the main portion of the Webinar presented by the third party. This approach is proven, and while it may take some effort to arrange, the results will be worth it. Before long your Webinars will be seen as adding true value to the decision cycles of many professionals, increasing your influence with them.

Generating Leads

This brings us to the generation of leads. Whether a Webinar has the effect of turning over immediate sales following the session or encourages viewers to put you on the short list when they make their purchase decisions, you've got a lead in hand. By running a well-executed Webinar that attracts attention, you can fill your lead pipeline to capacity. Your attendees are directly expressing interest in the topic, and they're saying as much directly to you. From here you should have a well-crafted plan to manage communications and help escort these folks to the final conversion. Your plan might have steps such as these, starting from when they sign up for the Webinar:

- Thank you e-mail reminding them of the date, time, and topic of the Webinar and who the expert speaker will be. Including a one-click way for them to add this to their Microsoft Outlook or Gmail calendar is always a nice touch, too. Keep this e-mail clean, simple, and easy to read. Bullet points work well here.
- Reminder e-mail 24 hours in advance of the event. Use the information captured during their sign up to personalize this e-mail with their names, and take the time to remind them that they signed up to "learn more about . . . " or to "discover ways to . . . " The goal here is to excite users about the Webinar and generate enthusiasm to attend. Again, skip any sales pitches and stay close to the point.
- This is optional, but I always like to send a quick reminder a couple of hours before the Webinar is going to start. This e-mail can be extremely short and to the point, such as, "This is a friendly reminder that the Webinar on [topic] which you signed up for will begin in two hours. Please click here to join the session when ready."

At this point I'll remind you that in each e-mail, you should include a link to the Webinar itself. You have no way of knowing which communication users will open to join the Webinar, so make sure the link to join the session appears in all communications prior to the session.

- After the session wraps up, a "Thanks for attending" e-mail is acceptable. Use this opportunity to thank attendees for their time, to suggest ways they can learn more, and to invite them to contact you for further information. If there is a special offer associated with the Webinar, this is a chance to remind them about it and about any deadlines that are involved.

Now that you've completed this cycle with users, it's time to migrate their e-mail addresses onto the "future Webinars" list. This is the list you will use to send out information about upcoming Webinars. Don't worry about the topic either. Let users decide for themselves if they are interested in attending. Use these communications to bring value to users' in-boxes, thus cementing your position as a valuable information contributor in their world. The name of the game here is to build credibility, because credibility sells.

Now let's take a look at some of the things that make a good Webinar a great Webinar.

How to Make a Great Webinar

Here are a few suggestions for going from "good" to "great":

- Remember the teacher you had who made learning fun? We all had one, and you need to ensure that your Webinars embody that same spirit. Stay away from dry and bland. Don't be afraid to spice up the discussion. Make learning fun for your viewers—they are far more likely to remember you this way. Inject some humor and show them you are witty, or draw a parallel between two seemingly unrelated topics in a humorous manner.
- Be negative, it works. . . . Don't be afraid to embrace the negative spin. By showcasing information on "How to fail . . . " or "Worst ways to . . . ," you help people zone in on areas of failure. Your lists form the nucleus of success, because if people know what not to do, they can avoid making mistakes. You can broach sensitive topics without being crass. You can be provocative without being rude. So find the line and cozy up to it. Having a different point of view on things, and expressing it, isn't always a bad thing.

- Keep the content simple and the presentation basic. If you keep the content simple, users won't struggle with understanding it, thus making them feel smarter. This is an obvious way to influence folks. Another benefit of this simplicity, though, is that it will not distract from the message being presented. Most successful Webinars showcase only the smallest of logos in one lower corner—the audience is not there to see your brand, but to learn and be influenced, though they might not fully realize that second part. This is a good thing, though, as it's your job to influence them.
- Use lists. They are an excellent way to share information quickly and to allow users to easily capture the essence of the slide or segment. Lists also force you to streamline and cut out the fat. By focusing your content into lists, you trim away all the excess verbiage and present attendees with exactly what they want to know.
- Provide value and you will be remembered. Take a long hard look at what you consider "proprietary" information. Just because you pulled the documentation together doesn't mean the information is truly unique. There will be plenty of times when you will be able to share your information freely without giving away secrets, and, by doing so, you will demonstrate a desire to help people learn and understand. This forms the basis of their trust in you and your products and services. If you go just a bit deeper and share a bit more than your competitors share, you will secure conversions.

Webinars are true standouts in the effort to increase conversions. There are an endless variety of ways to record and showcase them, but your goal should be to strike a balance between suggestive selling and education. If you lean toward education, you'll be in safe territory. One last tip on Webinars . . . attend as many as you can and look for ways to make your own stand out. The time spent in this effort will be worth it.

Next in line, we'll take a look at banner advertising and how to position your campaigns to help increase conversions.

7

Internet Advertising Banners:
A Tried and True Method

WE'VE ALL SEEN banner ads. In fact, almost every site has either had them in the past or has them currently. Banner ads come in all sizes and shapes these days, and seem to be integrated everywhere online. The most common ads are banners across the top of a Web page, or an almost square ad just below the header area. They remain an excellent way to monetize a Web site, and if you optimize your own banners carefully, you can have highly effective campaigns that deliver prequalified users to your Web site.

It might seem that the way to get banners on a Web site is by contacting a Web site directly, but this is not so in many cases. Many medium and large Web sites sell ad space through networks, and even smaller sites are starting to follow this trend. Lower costs and headaches on their end are the main reasons. You can, however, still find lots of sites willing to sell you ad space. Even sites displaying no ads at all may agree to place your ad. They simply may never have thought to try this before you contacted them.

Converting users who arrive on your Web site after clicking on banners requires a dedicated focus on optimizing your banners. Refining the message and testing multiple versions is the best way to figure out which works best. You must choose your placements and banner sizes carefully as well. Don't be afraid to suggest new banner sizes to sites either. Larger banners perform better, as do banner locations "above the fold" on a Web page, so seek these placements.

Increasingly, banner advertisers are turning to day-parting as a way to increase click-through rates. Day-parting allows you to show your ads only when you know traffic on a site is high, and you stand a better chance of seeing traffic more likely to convert. For example, if the site where your banner will appear is frequented by users during their evenings, when they are home from work, your banners can be set to show only during those hours. If the locations from which you are buying banner ad placements allow day-parting, there is usually no increased cost to you, so it's worth it to ask. Combine this practice with dedicated landing pages tailored to match the message your banners promote and you have a very refined approach to banner advertising. Now let's take a look at your options in more detail.

■ ■ ■ Networks

A network can be thought of as a collection of Web sites across which banner advertising appears. Indeed, many Web sites that you visit every day are part of an ad network. It's not something that is openly advertised, nor is there any reason to do so. By being part of an ad network, a Web site can increase its ad yield rate (meaning how much it gets paid for each instance that a user visits a Web page and your banner is displayed). If a user refreshes the Web page, that's a second impression. It removes the burden of managing the ad units itself, and limits the Web site's need to invest time in the entire process of finding advertisers. On the surface, joining an ad network might seem like just the ticket for a Webmaster. Ad revenue rolls in, while the work is limited to placing a small bit of code on your site one time.

There are, however, some limits to keep in mind.

There are basically two types of networks: tier one and tier two. As you might expect, things are typically better on tier one networks, "better" being subjective, though I'll try to break down the difference between the two tiers a bit more thoroughly. On a tier one network, there is full disclosure about the Web sites on which an advertiser's ad will appear, and the rates tend to be higher. As a result, you tend to find more well-known Web sites participating. On tier two networks, while ad rates are lower, there is less transparency about where an advertiser's ad might appear. This is usually due to the practice of buying remnants, which are ad impressions left unsold either on individual Web sites or across networks.

The real downside of joining a tier two ad network, as an advertiser, is that you may not know where your ads are appearing. And since we are judged by the company we keep, this could spell trouble if your ad were to show up on a less than desirable Web site. Just to be clear here, I'm not suggesting your ad *would* immediately show up on adult or gambling Web sites if you join a tier two network. Just know that the ad you spent time and money crafting *might* be shown to an entirely inappropriate and/or unresponsive audience. That's the downside here—a waste of your money.

Today, many networks offer pay-for-performance models, meaning you only pay when an action is taken. If the action is "click the banner and visit my Web site," then you pay per click. If the action is a conversion or sale, then you only pay for that action, not the traffic alone, which is preferable because you can easily track the ROI of any campaign you run this way. You can then adjust as needed the time of day the ads run. If allowed by the network, you could also shift between Web sites in the network and opt to introduce improved ads to try to increase your results.

As always, there's a trade-off here. If you choose to simply pay for traffic, you'll get better rates. If you specify a conversion, rates will increase. This is where understanding your own Web site and optimizing it for conversions makes a difference. Investing time in simplifying the path users take to make a purchase, in essence, optimizes the conversion process altogether.

Individual Web Sites: Direct Buying

Buying your ads directly from Web sites themselves can be difficult work. Most Web sites, in an effort to minimize the amount of work on their end, opt to participate in networks. Thus your only opportunity to advertise with them is by going through those networks. Once involved with a network, a Web site will not be allowed to also sell ad space on its own—one condition of joining a network is that the network controls the ad space.

Many of the larger Web sites join an ad network, so a great place to look for ad space for a direct buy is within niche Web sites. On any given topic there are tens, hundreds, and sometimes thousands of Web sites catering to the common interests of potentially millions of online users.

You name the topic, there are Web sites online loaded with information about it. Now, many of these sites tend not to have the highest quality in design and layout, but that should matter little to you. Remember, your overriding goal should be conversions. Do you really care if the site showing your banner is a plain html Web site with basic black text on white pages? No, you don't. The only thing you should care about is traffic. Does the site have any? Can the site owners provide you proof, either in the form of past reports and traffic numbers, or with a test flight of your ads? Posting your ad for one week should be long enough to test the exposure for value. With these smaller, niche sites, don't be afraid to ask. Worst case, they say no. Best case, you get the flight of test ads running and see for yourself. For many niche Web sites it's unlikely the site is the sole focus of the Webmaster or whichever individual you'll be dealing with. In many cases the Web site is a sideline or hobby, so you should remember to be flexible about things like actual start dates, whether the Web site returns e-mails immediately, and the ad sizes it can accommodate.

It's no secret that blogging has exploded, so look to blogs as opportunities for exposure for your banners too. Blogging is an entirely different world than the one inhabited by regular Web sites, so be ready for a difference when you get involved. Generally speaking, bloggers care more about credibility than profits, though this trend is starting to change. While you might want to place your ad on a particular blog, finding the owner, talking to him or her, and, in some cases, convincing that person can take time and effort. In the world of blogs, you might be better served starting high up and trying to work your way back down. In other words, you should look for ad space on popular, well-known blogs for your products and services before seeking out smaller ones. Usually these more well-known blogs will already be set for advertising and be accustomed to dealing with advertisers, so working out a solid plan that drives converting traffic to your site will be easier.

Take the time to figure out who the informal leaders are in the niche. Do the research. Participate in conversations on blogs and Web sites, and then approach the most appropriate ones about advertising with them. Bloggers and niche site operators tend to be very connected to their users and communities, and they are keenly aware that whomever they promote reflects on their own sites.

In many cases you will find that when you purchase banner ads, you tend to get more than you paid for. By setting expectations around performance up front and by clearly communicating with the site about performance each week during the campaign, you can have productive discussions once the campaign is over. If performance was better than expected, write another check and keep going. If it was lower than expected, ask the Web site/blog to work out another arrangement. In exchange for another month of advertising, sites will usually give you more exposure.

When I was running banner ad campaigns, if any were returning 10 to 20 percent below my expected success rates, I'd often ask the Web site for another 10 to 20 percent on top of the contractual agreement. It didn't matter whether it was impressions or clicks the Web site was charging for. The Web site usually agreed to help me try to meet my overall goals. Unless a Web site is totally sold out of ad inventory, it will usually accommodate this request after the first month's results are in. You do need to be realistic and honest, though. The worst thing you can do is to build a reputation for trying to swindle Web sites out of traffic and users by pretending your banner ad campaign results were much lower than they actually were. If your results truly were that bad, don't sign on for a second month. Period. Try another site.

■ ■ ■ Online Advertising: How to Get Conversions

Now is the time to discuss how you can target customers with your banner ads. Unlike text-based advertising or some social media marketing, which rely on written text, banner advertising is visual. A picture often really is worth a thousand words, and in the visual environment of banner advertising, you can capitalize on this. We are drawn to glossy images of products we seek, so, where appropriate and legal, you should try to incorporate product images into your banners. You'll need to be creative here, as banner sizes, while diverse, do follow a more or less standard pattern.

Table 7.1 shows a list of the most common sizes in use today—sizes are in pixel x pixel measurements.

300 × 250 – Medium Rectangle
250 × 250 – Square Pop-Up
240 × 400 – Vertical Rectangle
336 × 280 – Large Rectangle
180 × 150 – Rectangle
300 × 100 – 3:1 Rectangle
720 × 300 – Pop-Under
468 × 60 – Full Banner
234 × 60 – Half Banner
88 × 31 – Micro Bar
120 × 90 – Button 1
120 × 60 – Button 2
120 × 240 – Vertical Banner
125 × 125 – Square Button
728 × 90 – Leaderboard
160 × 600 – Wide Skyscraper
120 × 600 – Skyscraper
300 × 600 – Half Page Ad

Table 7.1. Banner Sizes

Keep in mind that while this list represents most of the currently popular banner sizes, there are sure to be more, depending on how Web sites are set up. There are also no hard and fast rules around which Web sites use which sizes. Most Web sites online today have been experimenting for years to understand which ad size performs best for their advertisers. When in doubt, bigger usually performs better. While statistics vary around effective reporting across banner sizes, the fact remains that larger ads are seen better on today's busy Web site pages.

The goal for you is twofold. Generate the click action to deliver the users to your Web site, and then get them to convert.

The first part is tricky to control. There are some adjustments you should be making with your banners ads, such as integrating animation (Adobe's Flash or Microsoft's Silverlight products are great for this) and maximizing the space and time of exposure to ensure that the "call to action" is clearly seen by users. Keep the graphics crisp and light so that the ad will load and animation will play quickly. You'll need to do your research in advance to crack this nut, though, so don't expect this to happen automatically. You will still need to create multiple versions of the ad, with different items shown, so you can track the success of which ads generate more clicks and conversions. While time-intensive, and a bit costly, if you farm out creative development, the data this type of testing can provide is worth the effort.

You'll have the physical space limitations to contend with as well. If you buy ad space that's smaller (468 × 60, for example), your real estate is more limited than it would be with a larger banner (336 × 280, for example). You will have smaller images, smaller text, and a smaller chance of being seen by users as they scroll through pages. Try to negotiate deals that allow for more exposure through the use of larger banner ads. Even if a Web site doesn't have a bigger ad unit in place on its site, ask for it. Many sites will redesign pages if there is enough demand for a new ad size.

It is very important to ensure that your ad features a solid call to action. Make sure you clearly define the action you want users to take. "Buy today," "Enroll now," "Join today," "Click for your discount," "Sign up now," and "Contact us today" are all valid calls to action. With some creativity and testing, you'll discover other phrases and words that drive action. Keep track of the top performers and use them until the results start to fall off. At that point recycle other past top-performing phrases and words.

Another noteworthy trait about banner advertising is that it goes stale rather quickly. Unlike text ads, which are expected to say the same thing for long periods of time, banner ads need to be constantly refreshed to remain effective. Again, watching your stats will help you determine when an ad unit is starting to lose steam. When I used to purchase advertising, I'd typically view between three and four weeks of top performance for an ad. After that, performance fell and I needed fresh material. As users frequent a Web site and begin to see the same ads over and over, the ads lose effectiveness; although users might never have clicked on the ads in the first place, the ads begin to blend in to the background after a while. When that happens, any potential effectiveness is lost.

Now, by using rich media (Adobe's Flash or Microsoft's Silverlight) to build you banners, they can be much more fluid and thus more eye-catching. Because the human eye is built to notice moving things, you can use this trait to your advantage. Be sure to create clean graphics that move fast enough to attract attention but not so fast that users might miss the action. You generally have around 5 to 15 seconds to engage the interest of users when they view your ad, so make the most of it. Get to the point quickly and get that call to action working for you.

Assuming all of your efforts align and your banners are driving users to your site, what can you do to turn those clicks into conversions? A good place to start is by ensuring that each ad you have that drives users to a product or service lands them on a dedicated sales page for that product or service. Nothing kills conversions like dropping users looking for a new coffeemaker on your home page and making them search the site for coffeemakers. The "Back" button is a whole lot easier to use than searching through an unfamiliar Web site.

Just as in search engine marketing, whether paid or organic, there's an ebb and flow at work here. If your ads drive traffic but users are frustrated by the Web site experience, they'll leave. Over time, the low performance around conversions will become more obvious. As the site owner, you likely won't buy another ad campaign on the same site, thinking the traffic on the site "just doesn't convert." Don't be so fast to judge, though. Ask the Web site for its stats on your ads. The numbers won't match up (they never do because of variances in reporting systems), but the trends will shed some light on things. If its stats show a lot of users clicking the ads and you're not seeing conversions, this confirms the tracking on both ends is accurate and helps you understand the issue is on your Web site.

Now, it's entirely possible to see "garbage" traffic from Web sites—traffic that simply doesn't convert, but this is where watching your own analytics helps. By cross-referencing your own stats to determine the amount of time users who show up via your banner ads spend on your Web site, you'll begin to see a picture of how they're interacting with your site. Look for clues in the paths they take when navigating your site. Look for clues in the entry page that lands them there (this should be the dedicated landing page for the banner ad, as you'll remember). Do users spend time on that dedicated landing page? Are they interacting with it? Or do they almost immediately click off through your navigation to another section of your site?

By watching the data closely, you will find clues to help you refine your landing pages and develop your systems to capture those folks who don't convert on the first try. If you see a lot of users clicking a banner for a particular product, but they go on to purchase something else from your Web site, then maybe you should swap ads to showcase the other item.

Users clicking on a banner ad with a clear call to action in it are, most likely, interested in exploring that action further. Your job is now to make it as easy as possible for them to follow through. The speed of your site will matter, as will the number of steps in your shopping cart and checkout system. The type of personal information you ask for will matter. Even something as simple as enabling a check box to autopopulate "billing address information" from the "shipping address information" already captured can make a difference. Ultimately, converting users who came to you via a banner ad is little different than converting them from most other sources. The key lies in the details.

■ ■ ■ Banner and Text Advertising: When Selling Ads on Your Site

For some Web sites, the end goal is page views—just getting folks "thumbing" through the Web site. Essentially, these Web sites are selling ad space, as opposed to a specific service or product. This increasing page view count exposes the users to more and more ads, one of which they might well act on. Google's AdSense (adsense.google.com) program is a great way to get a site monetized with ads related to your content—which is always the goal. The only way to win is to show users what they want, when they want it. While not the only program of its kind online, the AdSense program is a proven entity, and Google reliably pays out money to those who are enrolled in the program and meet the requirements set forth in its guidelines. You might think this is an obvious point, but many people have been burned participating in dubious affiliate programs where the other party reaped the reward, and the Web site owner was out all that time and effort.

Google has done a great deal of work tracking ad placements for its clients' Web pages and understanding which locations generate more clicks. The Google image in Figure 7.1 is a "heat map" that illustrates where ads should be placed to optimize clicks. This information has been collected from a long history in Google's database and is generally considered the accepted best practices for advertising placements. As usual, you will get optimal results by starting from a position such as those suggested here and then testing to figure out what your users respond to best. In the heat map shown here, darker shades represent areas proven to show increased click-through rates. In short, place your ads in the darkest spots, as they perform best in these locations. This is a general rule of thumb, though—a starting point—so test, test, test.

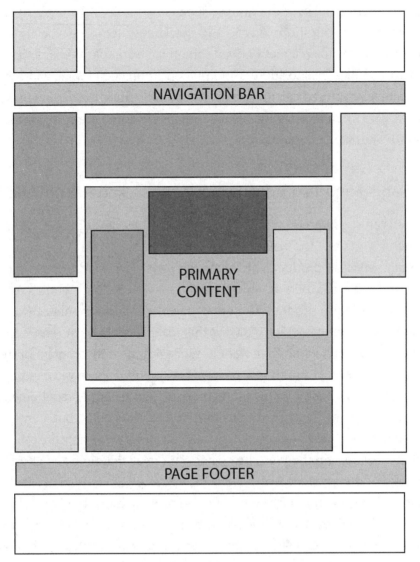

Figure 7.1. Heat map

The AdSense program allows you a great deal of control over how the ads look, and you should use this to your advantage. The best place to start is by building ads that blend with the Web site as much as possible. When you've had such ads in place for a while, you can begin experimenting to see what changes move the results up or down. You might discover that your users don't even see the ads that blend into the background. You might need to switch to ads that contrast with your pages to make them stand out.

Ultimately, though, your ability to control these ads is limited. While you can block certain ads (ideal when you don't want competing sites showing up on your own), there is little you can do to select which ads are shown. Google does a lot of work to make sure the right ads are shown at the right time and that the ads shown match the content of the page they are being shown on. The end result is a handy way to get started in monetizing your Web site. The good news is that there are no minimum requirements for traffic. Google doesn't care if you have one visitor or one million.

Sometimes you might also notice ad banners rotating through your inventory from the Google AdSense system. Some advertisers want to be able to show banners, and while generally not as effective at generating the click action everyone wants, image-based banner ads will stand out in a space typically populated with text links. You can opt to turn these off, which you might choose to do given that text ads typically have higher click-through rates (CTRs) and you are paid based on those clicks.

Google's AdSense system also allows you to select the size, shape, and number of ads that appear in a given ad unit. This makes the overall system more conducive to placements in a wide range of areas and applications. From blogs to traditional Web sites to community forums, AdSense has ad formats that integrate and work well. Figure 7.2 shows some AdSense ads blended in one of my own Web sites.

Figure 7.2. AdSense ad

This ad is very effective, as it cleanly meshes with the main site navigation. While some might think this sort of tactic is misleading to users, the fact is, it works. In the business of monetizing Web sites, you need to test, test, and test again. Over time you will find a balance between what users will accept and what brings in revenue. This particular ad isn't even the highest performer for the Web site. That status is reserved for the bigger ads.

Since we've touched on the topic of size, allow me to confirm that it indeed *does* matter—at least in terms of ads. The rule is, "Bigger is usually better." Ad systems such as AdSense will limit the sizes for you, so your choice is really which of *their* sizes you choose. That decision is often made for you by the layout of the Web site and the pages themselves. You can always go the simple route and stack a bunch of ads above your content, but the flip side to this excellent ad exposure is a less than ideal user experience. By requiring new users to your site to scroll down to find your content, they may simply opt to leave and look at another Web site. In Figure 7.3 we can see how the ads drive the content lower on the page, forcing users to scroll before finding content of value to them.

This example brings to mind a few areas I'd examine in greater deal if the site were mine. First is the obvious one of too many ads pushing the content of the Web site much lower on the page. Next there's the issue of the images themselves. They all add time to the loading process for the Web page, so the page takes longer to load up, thus slowing and negatively affecting the user experience. A small annoyance associated with this loading of images is that most of the page content will render before the ad images appear. When the ads themselves start to load up, the page begins to jump down. Users might start reading content on the page only to suddenly see that content disappear or move down. As more ads load, the process is repeated, frustrating users even further.

Now, before we condemn a Web site for this approach, there is more to look at here than just the user experience. While important, the effect on the user experience needs to be considered in conjunction with other issues facing the Webmaster. As the site owner, you are faced with the decision of which ad goes where. In the quest to monetize the Web site, having many advertisers paying lower per month rates often makes sense. But how do you showcase all the ads, allowing decent exposure for each one and making the advertisers feel as though they are receiving value for their dollars?

The example shown in Figure 7.3 is one such compromise. Given the focused niche of the site, it's not an altogether bad compromise either. Most users of the site are intensely interested in the topic, so the ads are less likely to distract them. In fact, given how tightly matched the ads are to the topic, and how varied each ad is, it's a decent showcase of alternative options for users to browse. I'd even go so far as to say that in this example those ads provide direct value to the users of the site by allowing them direct access to other Web sites that support their hobby.

Figure 7.3. Ad positioning

One option to improve this space issue and shorten the page would be to install an ad rotation system. Such systems enable you to rotate ads in one predefined space. You set the specification that all ads must be a certain size, the advertisers deliver (or you make their ads for them), and you set the ads into rotation. An even rotation ensures that everyone gets the same amount of exposure each month. In this way, you effectively reduce the amount of space the ads take up by rotating multiple ads through the same spot. With such a system, the site depicted in Figure 7.3 could reduce the number of stacked ads from eight layers to three. The site has 21 ads showcased, so it could easily accommodate all of them in rotation. The trouble encountered here is that the ads are all different sizes. However, most ad systems can handle this, provided you specify the space to accommodate the largest size. Smaller ads will fit into larger ad spaces, but the opposite is not true. If you put a larger ad into a smaller space, the larger ad will be visually cut off and therefore incorrect.

Selling the Ads

Since we've already discussed how you would encourage users to click on the ads, let's go over how you manage to sell the ads in the first place. Getting users to click on your banner ads requires that you place the right message or image in front of them at the right time—which is whenever they are on the Web site while your ad appears there.

If your goal is to sell banner ad space on your Web site, your job is no less difficult. You need to ensure optimal placement for your advertisers, which means striking a balance between the user experience and the advertiser experience. This can be difficult because, while your advertisers will happily tell you exactly where on a page they want their banners to appear, your users won't contact you to say they don't like the ads there. They will simply start going to other Web sites. However, if you follow the heat map diagram shown in Figure 7.1, you'll be on the right path for a solid starting point.

Another point to consider is size. Larger ads perform better for advertisers, so you should seek ways of designing your pages so that they can accommodate these larger ad sizes. Don't be afraid to offer smaller sizes; just be thoughtful about where you place them and how you price their value relative to your larger, more prominent ads. Often, Web sites throw these into banner ad deals at no charge for advertisers willing to purchase their more expensive ad slots.

When selling banners, it's important to be realistic. Always be honest with potential advertisers about your volume of traffic. Trying to impress them with inflated numbers will backfire when their ads fail to perform. Unless you have millions of users on your site every day, no one is likely to pay your $10,000 per month for ad space. Given how trackable everything is today, you'll be better served by starting out with modest ad rates for the first few advertisers who pony up. You should watch their results and see if you can use their success to increase rates slightly for a new advertiser. Using Google AdSense is a great way not only to monetize your site but also to define ad spaces, test them for effectiveness, and track what ECPM rates you could start with (ECPM measures the effective cost per each thousand page views). All this information will be provided in the reporting system used, such as the one provided with the Google AdSense platform.

Rarely do advertisers talk and compare notes on ad rates, so this is a legitimate route to increase your yield from these spaces over time. Just be sure that you can justify the increases if you are asked about them. Although advertisers rarely share this information, it does happen. For that reason, you should also have a plan in mind for advertisers who started out with you at a lower rate. Keep them at their lower rate until you see revenues increase from other advertisers. Then you might want to approach them and offer a locked-in rate for the next six months or so, politely explaining that as traffic has increased on your site, so has demand for ad space, driving your ad rates higher. Give them the option to renew at a new rate after the extended grace period. Another option might be to transition them to smaller ad units (or even to text links) for their current ad rates. The main point here is that you plan for the changeover and communicate with them. Upsetting advertisers is not a good way to keep the ad dollars flowing.

Banner advertising can be a very effective way to deliver traffic to your Web site. Given that the nature of the ads is highly visual, you can also ensure that users are prequalified before they even hit your site, helping your efforts to convert. Like many areas of online marketing, banner advertising is best served with a big side order of testing.

Next we'll examine social media in depth and look at how to position yourself as a thought leader and how to derive conversions from this effort. Social media is all about positioning, contribution, and intent. Get the mix right and users will follow you religiously. Make a rookie mistake up front and you could hurt your brand.

8

Social Networking and Blogging: The New Way to Get Conversions

SOCIAL MEDIA AND social networking are still relatively new ways to reach customers and draw them to your site. It seems that every day there is a new social space to join. But think carefully before jumping on the latest bandwagon, or, for that matter, about joining the oldest bandwagons.

You need to have a clearly defined plan around social media or you could make simple mistakes that may negatively impact your brand perception. Know exactly what your goals are before diving in and invest in ways to track how your exposure affects your number of conversions. Deriving conversions from the tens of millions of people participating in social media Web sites requires a deft touch, a smooth presentation, and well-honed instincts. Participating in social media will have you rescheduling your calendar to make time, but the rewards in terms of credibility and reputation-building can easily pay off. Never before has it been so easy to reach so many people in order to influence how they see you and your products or services and to interact with them.

■ ■ ■ How to Get Started

The social environment online is a unique area in which to pursue conversions. While much of the activity on social Web sites is exactly that, social users can still be influenced toward purchase decisions. One of the most important aspects to understand when participating in social media is to avoid overt, direct sales tactics. Much of the social environment exists in an informal unstructured manner. Showing up in this space and doing a hard-sell for your product will, at best, be met with silent dismissal, or, at worst, with a direct backlash against your Web site and product. Users engaged in social activities online need to be approached in a more thoughtful manner.

You must clearly define your goals and make a plan for how to achieve them. When engaging in social media, as with any other space, your goal should be concrete and attainable. As examples, here are goals that are appropriate for the social media environment: (a) building brand awareness, (b) tracking brand awareness, and (c) driving sales. Most businesses think that by simply opening a Twitter account and posting occasional content, they are participating in driving awareness and sales. While opening such accounts is the first step to marketing in social media, understanding how to use your presence in this area is critical for your long-term success.

Social media can be summed up in one word: engagement. The primary goal of marketers using social media is to encourage active engagement around a brand or product name. This active engagement can take the form of mentions (which is when someone else mentions your username or business in a conversation you did not originate) and discussions about your business, or it can take the form of actual conversions, some even involving you. You'll have a long road to travel, though, between opening an account and seeing your users' active engagement pay off. Many people think that by using social media they will find a shortcut to driving awareness and conversions; however, the reality is that, as with so many things, engaging in social media takes a lot of time and effort.

■ ■ ■ How to Get Conversions

The clearest proven path to success in social media is to engage your audience. By being an active contributing member of the community, you can bring your expert knowledge to the table. In this manner you will be seen as an authority in your field, and thus build credibility. In social media this credibility is gold.

It's this credibility that enables you to lead users toward your end goal of driving conversions.

The first step you should take in any social environment is to customize your space with an eye toward conversions. On a Web site such as Twitter, this can be done by simply altering the background image in your profile. Keep things simple and avoid too many images and dark colors. The impression users should have of your presence is: clean, clear, crisp, and professional—with nothing to hide. White is known to subliminally emphasize all these qualities, while black does the opposite. Green is often associated with wealth, as the "color of money," while red tends to incite passion. If your goal is conversions, which it should be, then you must be careful to ensure that your profile reflects your business's personality and not necessarily your own. Users want to know they can trust a business, and, in most cases, are less interested in the individual(s) behind it.

For example, your business presence in a place like Twitter should be clean, professional, inviting, and helpful. This might seem boring when your goal is to engage in exciting conversations and show a dynamic involvement in the world of your potential clients. Save the silly images, links to your favorite music, and funny observations for a separate, personal Twitter account, and set that account to "Private."

When you open your business account, take advantage of the unique marketing opportunity to use your profile to showcase your business. You should approach the profile in each social space as a chance to sum up who you are and what you can do. To that end, it's also important to always link to your own Web site in the profile so that viewers can click directly to it. When you fill in the description, keep the sales pitches out of it. Use this space simply to describe the products and services you offer. Remember that generating conversions from social media is about subtle suggestion and not about overt sales pitches.

If you take the time to carefully plan your social media activities, you can outline clearly defined targets, which will lead to success. Your plan may start quite simply as a calendar of events. Participating in social media requires that you engage thoughtfully in the conversations going on around you. If you are a subject matter expert, this will be easy, as you can slip into and out of conversations, lending your expertise as needed. By ensuring that you plan your participation on a regularly scheduled basis, you can teach users a pattern of engagement. Over time they will come to understand when you will be around. Even when you're not around, these users will continue to interact on your behalf by creating conversations that mention you or your products by name or by recommending you to others in the community.

Each social media space has a uniquely different personality. Each one attracts different people looking for different things. As an example, Digg.com is known to be intolerant of those who practice search engine optimization. Digg is a social space where users post topics of interest to themselves, in their own accounts. You can choose to share your postings with the rest of the community, and, because of that, Digg users have had to endure a litany of spam posting from shady search optimizers seeking to extract value from having their links appear. Generally speaking, most users on Digg view search engine optimization as a spam tactic. While I do not share that opinion, I certainly understand how people can be left with this impression. Some people have simply grown intolerant of anyone appearing to drop links for the purposes of search optimization, so much so, in fact, that users often find themselves shunned and ridiculed within the community if they are perceived to be involved in this activity.

I mention this not to single out Digg as problematic but to clearly illustrate one type of personality in a social space. Other social arenas such as LinkedIn, Facebook, Twitter, and Newsvine.com all have unique personalities that you need to understand in order to interact with their communities in a productive manner. If you seek to make a positive impression in a social space such as LinkedIn, you need to understand the main focus of the site. The main focus of LinkedIn is business networking, so you should approach each interaction from that angle. Trying to always be funny or glib when answering questions at LinkedIn won't win you many friends in the long run. This is where taking the time to do your research pays dividends. By understanding the personality of each community, you can alter your approach so as to be as helpful and useful to the community as possible. By bringing value to each community in a way unique to each community's personality, you will be viewed as a credible contributing member.

In Appendix 2, you will find a list of some of the most common online social communities available today. While not exhaustive, the list covers many of the top global sites. To locate social spaces and Web sites, turn to your favorite search engine and start placing specific queries around the phrases "community," "posting forum," "discussion forum," "groups," or "discussion boards," plus phrases related to the topic you seek. Here is an example: to find a social community in which to participate in conversations centered around the topic of photography, I would turn to Bing.com or Google.com and query "photography discussion forum." The results would look like the depictions in Figures 8.1 and 8.2, and would give me a good starting point for further research.

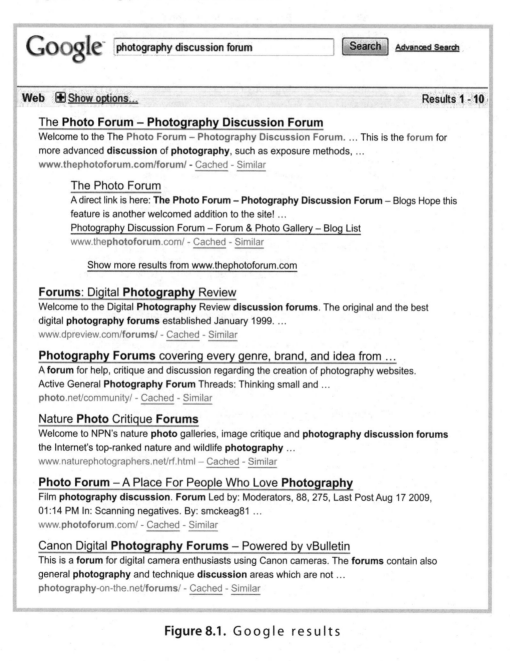

Figure 8.1. Google results

**bing**

photography discussion forum 🔍

ALL RESULTS   1-10 of 58,3000,000 results – Advanced

SEARCH HISTORY

photography discussion
forum

See all

Clear all | Turn off

The Photo **Forum** – **Photography Discussion Forum**

The **Photography forum** with photo hints, tips, advice and critique. **Discuss**
everything from differentcamera models including digital cameras, SLR's and more.
www.thephoto**forum**.com/**forum** – Cached page

Forums: Digital **Photography** Review

Discussion Forums. Welcome to the Digital **Photography** Review **discussion**
forums. The originaland the best digital **photography forums** established January 1999.
www.dpreview.com/**forums** – Cached page

The Photo **Forum**

A direct link is here: The Photo **Forum** – **Photography Discussion**
Forum – Blogs Hope this feature is another welcomed addition to the site!
0 Replies | 454 Views
www.thephoto**forum**.com – Cached page

World **Photography Forum** – **Photography** & Camera **Discussion Forum**

An online **discussion forum** and gallery for all things **photography**. Upload images to
our free gallery for helpful critique or **discuss photography** technique in our free gallery.
www.world**photographyforum**.com – Cached page

photography software – **photography Discussion Forum**

Photography discussion forum: **photography** software … My questions are regarding
software. The 2 more expensive options I'm considering are Adobe Photoshop CS3 or
Adobe Lightroom2 …
www.amazon.com/tag/**photography**/**forum**?
cd**Forum**=Fx1INORLOON6TB3&cdThread=Tx3DR49A2QS9FSS – Cached page

Photography Discussion – AudiWorld Forums

New! Use your Facebook, Google, AIM & Yahoo accounts to securely log into this site,
click logo to login
forums.audiworld.com/**forum**display.php?f=116 – Cached page

T1i – **photography Discussion Forum**

Photography discussion forum: T1i … New to it all, looking to get a T1i, any advise
on the "must haves"
www.amazon.com/tag/**photography**/**forum**?
cd**Forum**=Fx1INORLOON6TB3&cdThread=Tx3IFKTO6NBWXDL – Cached page

Figure 8.2. Bing results

As you can see, using different search engines brings back slightly different results. Using more than one search engine is an excellent way to ensure that you're not missing any opportunities. While it's easy to think that today's social media Web sites were the beginning of the social movement online, discussion forums and distribution lists began the social movement at almost the same time the Internet became widespread in the mid 1990s.

While the list in Appendix 2 gives an indication as to the breadth of social activity online, the depth is almost limitless. Couple any topic or keyword with the phrase "discussion forum" and thousands of viable results will be returned. While the rules of engagement will differ from group to group, in general if your attitude is one of being helpful and contributory, you will be welcomed and embraced by the community. It is always best to either read the rules fully before you begin participating or ask before you do things such as dropping links and sharing information about products or services. Often you will learn that there are dedicated areas for businesses to display their products and services in full view of the membership.

Further to this point—and we will discuss it more in an upcoming section— you may want to pursue a sponsorship opportunity with the community if you believe in the value of its membership. It is a wise move to assume that anything you may think of doing has already been done. That includes dropping random links to your own products or services—a favorite approach of spammers over the last five to six years. As a result of this activity, many communities either may block your attempt to drop links or simply edit your posts and remove them afterward. In some cases, dropping random links to your own products or services could lead to your being banned from the community.

One area where participating in the social spaces can benefit you is in using your link building for organic search marketing. By understanding what each community's rules are, you can engage in ongoing conversations in the community that will allow you to place links from the domain where a discussion is happening (the discussion forum, for instance) to your own Web site. By doing so, you create a Web of inbound links supporting your Web site. In most cases the value of these links is less than if they were to appear on a specific Web site and not in a discussion group area. While links from Web sites provide more overall value for search engine optimization purposes, there is also the value of direct traffic from the links you place in conversations in discussion forums. As readers see the link, they may click it and visit your Web site directly. As I said before, you should have the opportunity to supply a link in your profile that points people to your products and services; many communities have rules about this, though, so read them carefully and abide by them.

■ ■ ■ Microblogging

On microblogging sites such as Twitter, where space is at a premium, getting to the point quickly is a necessity. Be certain when you post content in such areas that you share a diverse selection of links with your followers. If you are perceived as supporting only your own business, users either will stop following you or simply ignore your actions. By sharing a wide selection of links related to your area of expertise, you prove your value to the community, and people pay attention to what you have to say. To help you post more efficiently and maximize the number of characters for your own message, be sure to use a service such as TinyURL or Bit.ly to shorten all of the URLs you wish to share. Such services compress long URLs into short, unique character sets. This allows you to use more of the maximum 140 or so characters for your own message.

Being actively engaged is the best chance you have at cultivating a deep and diverse following in social spaces. In an area such as Twitter, following popular figures often results in their following you. In Twitter, you receive updates by selecting whom you "follow." By choosing a person to "follow," you tell the system to share with you each post the other person makes. While this may not work with celebrities, those who are well known in specific industries usually return the favor. When users see your profile and notice the important people who are following you, they begin following you as well. By repeating this pattern you can build a relatively large group of followers by which you can spread your message many times each day.

Microblogging requires its own specific skill of wordsmithing. Often you are limited to a specific number of characters within which to get your message across. This limitation necessitates planning exactly what you are going to say to maximize each character. Services such as Bit.ly and TinyURL can go a long way toward helping ensure that you have the most number of characters available to get your message across.

Some other items to consider when in the microblogging space or even in the *macro*blogging space are specifically about the concept of "hooks"—catchy turns of phrase or points of view that attract attention. At this point I'd like to call out thanks to a friend for inspiring me with this list. Todd Malicoat (www.stuntdubl.com) is an expert at driving conversions from social media spaces, and a recent presentation he made clearly explained the concept of "hooks." While not the first to explain them, Todd has a deft touch at using them successfully. From his information, let's examine commonly used hooks in editorial writing:

- **Attack hook.** Openly attack someone's point of view. Post a response 180 degrees from the person's, but take care to think it through first.
- **Humor hook.** Create a point of view that is humorous. Look for a funny angle or note the obvious joke.
- **Contrarian hook.** Somewhat like the attack hook, this approach will see you disagreeing with noted experts. When experts make a post, don't be afraid to call them out. Pick apart their theories and thinking and pursue the experts openly. Be polite, but firm.
- **News hook.** By breaking news first and fast, you can create a name for yourself and drive results. Although popular, this approach is tough, and, because of the time difference, those on the East Coast usually get the jump on the West Coast folks by posting the day's latest news first. Nevertheless, striving to uncover news and "break a story" can get you recognized quickly.
- **Resource hook.** If you show users that you are the best resource by providing useful links, they will respond. Be willing to gather other resources and share them openly in your social spaces.
- **Ego hook.** This is a big one, as it is driven by people's primary motivations for recognition. If you want recognition yourself, do something newsworthy. If you suspect others of doing this, call them on it. Better yet, set things up so you can help them get the recognition. They get the recognition and they owe you one.

- **Picture/movie hook.** Noting a particular picture or movie is usually a popular way to gain recognition. Bringing forward information and linking or relating it to a popular movie or widely known image brings results.
- **Combination hook.** By combining hooks, you can create very effective viral campaigns. The "humor/movie" combination works well, as does the "contrarian/attack" hook combo.

If you take the time to practice using these hooks in a microblogging space, you can refine your skills to the point where most items you publish will be well received and acted upon by users. When you've reached this stage, you are ideally positioned to begin driving users to your Web site's products or services, which will see conversions increase. At this point you'll be viewed as a contributing expert member of the community, and users will listen to what you have to say. If you've crafted your personality correctly, your credibility will cause users to trust your motives. By not betraying that trust, you will continually reinforce their choice to do business with you.

■ ■ ■ Best Ways to Trigger Responses in Social Media Environment

Similar to hooks, where we encourage responses from users, social triggers are also ways to get users to take action. The following list discusses triggers, which are more basic than hooks to the human psyche and thus more powerful:

- Pride
    - Engages users for their own reasons. Maybe they want exposure, credit, adulation, status, or recognition of some form. Whatever they feel proud about can be a trigger.
    - Techmeme Leaderboard is an excellent example of activating a user's pride response. Users of this tracking site enjoy the competition to appear on the home page, with those attaining this status seen as something of a celebrity in the community.
    - Take advantage of how users respond to tokens of recognition. For example, they might like to receive a badge (such as a small image) that acknowledges them in some manner, which they can display in

their community profiles or on their own Web sites. You could leverage this by ensuring that select individuals in a social space receive badges recognizing their knowledge on a topic pertaining to your business. This is an excellent way to keep your brand top-of-mind and to have these informal leaders spread the word about your services or products.

- Citation
  - Call attention to something new or noteworthy.
  - Note a trend others may not have noticed or spoken about.
  - Discuss openly something controversial. You may need to pick a side for this approach, so be careful, because the side you pick may alienate users of your product who take the opposite position.
  - Come up with a unique perspective on something and leverage it. While your view doesn't have to be earth shattering, it should be unique and accurate.
- Anticipation
  - Drop links to new things. Be the first to break news, but be careful to do your research and get your facts straight.
  - Predict what big brands are going to do next. Don't be afraid to get this one wrong. How many lists do we see every January predicting what will happen in the year ahead? Rarely do people go back to check who was right and who was wrong. The goal here is to get people thinking about what you said.
  - Leverage excitement about something new and noteworthy in your user community. This is where growing your base of followers pays off. By reaching out to your base, you increase your ability to spread the word—your word—exponentially.
- Humor
  - Use humor judiciously. Since humor is very subjective, it can be a challenge to use it successfully. What you find humorous may be offensive to others. Keep in mind that most communities today are global in nature, so cultural factors often play a role in what's considered humorous and what's not. That being said, with practice, humor can be an excellent trigger point.

–Develop many good links by using humor as a trigger point. When users find something particularly humorous, they will spread links to the information quickly and in volume.

Use Subject Matter That Warrants Debate and Discussion

This is where planning what you are going to say comes into play. Being the person who sends Twitter updates about sitting in traffic will lead to users ignoring you. If you are thoughtful and respectful of the fact that you're using other people's time, and you focus on bringing valued content to the discussion each and every time, users will note this behavior and frequently look for your input.

Create an Experience

Use both pictures and words to tell the story. By creating content in this manner, the path users follow to get to your content won't matter. Whether it's 140 characters on Twitter or a blog post in a related community, when users know that the experience on your Web site is worth their time, they will come back again and again.

Everything Counts!

Keep the following things uppermost in your mind:

- Even the simplest and smallest of social interactions can pay dividends for you. A single tweet can make a huge difference.
- On your own Web site, be sure to activate systems, such as those handy clickable logos seen on most news Web sites, that allow users to reach out to their own social communities with one click. By enabling such behavior, users will spread immediate feedback to their networks about the things they interact with on your Web site. These networks can expose your products and services almost instantaneously to thousands of people.

■ ■ ■ You Get Back What You Put In

Although social areas may seem an excellent way to build links quickly and bring exposure to your services, it is important to remember that you get back what you put in. You need to ensure that your actions speak to your credibility, as they are a direct reflection on your business. For this reason alone, it is critical that you monitor your tone and responses while participating. Don't be baited into unproductive or negative conversations. As with any place where you'll meet people, there are a variety of personalities with whom you will interact. If you keep in mind that your goal is to drive conversions on your Web site, your conversations will be very clearly defined and productive. Everything you say should be filtered through the understanding that your main goal is to entice people to visit your Web site and conduct business with you.

While it might be tempting to view Facebook, Twitter, and MySpace as the "inventors" of social media, that honor actually extends back a few years to the advent of online communities and blogs. Although the conversations on those types of social spaces typically took longer to hold, they were truly the originators of mass social interaction and community building. Focused on an endless number of topics, blogs and communities fit into the concept of social interaction, but they deserve their own chapter, so we'll head there next.

9

Blogs and Communities: The Predecessors of Social Media

AS MENTIONED, NO conversation around social media marketing would be complete without referencing blogs and online communities. It is difficult to say which was the first blog or online community, but the fact is these types of Web sites are the forefathers of today's coolest online networking capabilities. Today's social Web sites owe their existence to these forms of initial peer-to-peer communications. While some of today's social spaces impose strict limitations on communication styles, these early social communication vehicles were, very simply, group discussions or one-on-one conversations. Indeed today you can find blogs and communities on just about any topic that may interest you. In fact, many people choose to operate businesses by focusing specifically around blogs or online communities. Blogs are often used to carry on a conversation with current or potential clients, as they are a great way to showcase your point of view. Let's take a quick look at each style and run through how to participate and encourage conversions.

■ ■ ■ Blogs

You can think of blogs as similar to one-on-one conversations. While today's blogs (perezhilton.com, boingboing.net, techcrunch.com, gizmodo.com) take the form of outright Web sites, the originals in this category were virtually devoid of advertising and sales messages. Today there are still dedicated groups of bloggers who absolutely abhor the idea of selling ads on their blogs. They view blogging as a very pure form of journalism. While there is certainly space for this point of view, our goal in this book is to drive conversions, so let's view blogs as a form of Web site with the desire to either host advertising or sell products or services directly through it. This does not mean your Web site should lack integrity, as contended by many bloggers. In fact, one of the main tenets of blogging is transparency. By being very clear and open with your readers, you build trust. When you establish that level of trust, you can begin to exert influence over your readers' purchases.

With the easy availability of stable blogging platforms, setting up and maintaining a blog is easier than ever. To start a blog today, you don't even need hosting space or a domain name. You can turn to spaces such as Wordpress or Blogger, and in a matter of minutes or hours you'll have a presence online that is capable of generating revenue. There are definitely benefits to managing your blog as a stand-alone Web site on your own hosting and with your own domain, but you have the option to start off otherwise.

As with other social interactions, you should strive for consistency, clarity, and a unique voice. You need to focus on what is special about your products or services and ensure that the voice you bring to your blog will help differentiate you in a sea of competition. And while it may be very lonely when you first start your blog, keep in mind that as your traffic grows, users will begin to participate by leaving comments via your blog's comment functionality (it's built into the software, so no worries about needing to know how to set anything up). You will wake up one morning and realize you're not alone anymore.

Well before this point you should prepare your Web site's layout for your sales plan. Take the time to decide what tone you want to convey with your words to ensure that every communication you post on your blog supports it. Do you want to be edgy? Do you want to be humorous? Do you want to write short posts or long posts? Do you want to be subtle or overt? These questions and more will help you determine the voice that best suits you. Keep in mind that as in any social setting, not everyone will like your style. This should not matter, however, as your goal is not to have every single person on your Web site; rather, it is to attract those whose thinking most closely aligns with yours. By doing this, you are basically prescreening your users to ensure that those more likely to convert will stay on your Web site. If they like your voice enough to follow your postings and communications, they're more likely to be influenced by what you have to say about products or services.

Changing Web site designs and themed layouts is very easy with today's blogging platforms. Be careful to choose blog themes that are easy on the eyes and have minimal images for quick upload times. By themes, I'm referring to the look and feel of your blog. Most software facilitates the easy downloading and installing of themes from third-party sources. (By installing and selecting a new theme, you can completely alter the appearance of your blog without losing any of the data you have.) These same basic rules that apply to any other Web site apply also to blogs. It will help if you understand some basic HTML or coding languages so you can manage your templates and edit them to include ads in specific locations.

Although Web sites and blogs have things in common, blogs are laid out differently from standard Web sites or e-commerce sites, and you have to take this into consideration as you plan your own strategy. For instance, blogs often generate significantly fewer page views than do standard Web sites. This is almost entirely due to the layout of blogs. Most blogs are set up to show a number of posts as you scroll lower on one page. On a regular Web site, each of these posts would be housed on an individual Web page, thus increasing the page view count. This can matter if your monetization plans are based around advertising. As with any Web site, more page views show more advertisements, increasing the chances of an ad being noticed and clicked on.

When you construct your blog, take advantage of the ability to add individual pages to the blog itself. Most systems such as Wordpress allow you to do so. While the ability to add pages might seem obvious, given the nature of blogs and how they publish content, there is a distinct difference between a post and a page. A post might appear on a particular page, as well as on a blog's main page. Blogs can also contain individual pages that are not posts, and these pages can be accessed through the blog's navigation. There are also a number of plug-ins available through communities such as those supported by Wordpress, which can make many tasks (publishing and editing content, approving user comments, tracking inbound links, and so on) around developing or maintaining your blog much simpler.

Blogs are an excellent way to develop a service-oriented conversation with potential clients. They are also an excellent way to keep current clients up-to-date on the latest news and information from your business. Because the general format allows you to post information and also allows users to comment on your posting, blogs are a great way to get feedback from your clients or potential clients before those potential clients make decisions. Many large companies today use blogs as a way to initiate interactive communication with loyal followers. They use it as a medium to test new ideas and concepts and offer rewards to those who keep up with company news and information.

If you have a service-based business, a blog is an excellent way to develop a presence online and to maintain a running conversation with those interested in a topic. Your blog can develop traffic the same that any other Web site does, and as your community grows and users comment on your postings, you'll develop an authority and be recognized for your expertise.

Converting with Blogs

While a blog may be considered a Web site, a Web site generally is not considered a blog. This may seem confusing, but Web sites are usually constructed so that more page views develop from each user who visits. The flip side to this difference, in favor of blogs, is that users visiting a blog often spend more time reading the content on the blog. Given that many blogs are set up so that the first page contains a number of individual posts, it's easy to see why users would spend more time on one page on a blog than they would on individual pages on a typical Web site. Blogs make it easy for users to consume more content on a given visit.

This means that blogs can be an excellent way to establish an expertise-based relationship with potential customers. As potential clients read through your blog and understand your point of view on a topic, they will build trust regarding your expertise. If the goal of your blog is to convert users into clients for your services, you should be offering them an easy way to communicate with you. The blog itself will enable users to leave comments, but you should also take steps to ensure that users can contact you easily. Set up a dedicated contact page with your name and all your contact information, and monitor it frequently. Be sure that users understand where you're located in relation to various time zones and give them the option to send you e-mails immediately with one click. Alternatively, you could place a form on your blog to capture users' e-mail addresses for use in building your own internal e-mailing list. Be careful with this idea, however, as there are rules on how it's supposed to be done. There are laws that govern how you can use a person e-mail address, so do some careful research before you send e-mails. A good practice when collecting e-mails is to enable a "double opt in" process by which users give you their addresses and you then confirm them by clicking a link that goes immediately back to the addresses. Such a process not only ensures that people signing up to receive your e-mails are aware of what they are doing, but it also protects you from being wrongfully accused of spamming.

If you've done your job and built trust with your users, they will reach out to you as an expert in your field. Often, bloggers offering services find it beneficial to participate in conversations on other blogs and social spaces. This can have the effect of driving users back to your blog and of reinforcing your expertise. It will also ensure that you can mention your blog and develop links to it in related communities and spaces.

If your blog is set up as a Web site—meaning the entire Web site is hosted on blog software with posts on the main page, contains other individual pages of content, and is designed to derive revenue from ad placements—then you need to get creative about where you place your ads. You also need to be careful about what your blog theme and layout look like. This is where a bit of programming or coding knowledge will go a long way to helping you place ads in exactly the right location. As mentioned earlier in the book, Google's AdSense program is an excellent way to start monetizing your Web site with advertisements. Based on its own history, Google provides the following diagram as a starting point (Figure 9.1). You may wish to consider this when placing ads in standard blog layouts.

Following the suggestions will help you understand how to structure your blog as well. While it may be tempting to have a vast Web page with many posts visible to users, if your goal is to generate revenue via advertisements on your page, you

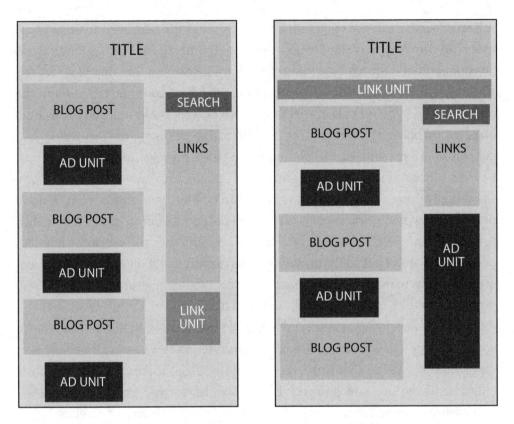

Figure 9.1. AdSense layout diagram

should devise your layout with a mind toward increasing page views. You can do this easily by simply limiting the number of posts that appear on the main page. This will encourage users to click to the next grouping of posts, generating another page view and showing more ads for you. Note the suggested placements of the ads in Figure 9.1 and you will see that as users finish reading a blog post, their eyes come naturally to the next piece of content, which is an advertisement. This is an excellent way to ensure that ads are actually being seen by your users. While many bloggers skip this step, carefully placing ads as suggested can have a positive effect on your ad revenue, so it's worth exploring.

Don't feel limited to AdSense either. You can combine it with other programs to generate different types of monetization options. If eBay has products related to your Web site's content, you may choose to stream a live feed of products available via eBay. The frequency of the updating from eBay ensures a stickiness of content, which will draw users back frequently, and when combined with a dedicated posting plan on your part, will ensure that users see value in visiting your blog on a regular basis. This type of approach—a scheduled posting plan combined with sticky, useful content—is a winner in generating loyalty. From this loyalty you will begin not only to gather a readership and page views but also to see links inbound to your Web site increasing and more traffic coming from search engines.

One critical point that should never be overlooked when you post on your blog concerns transparency. Whether you are selling services or monetizing through advertisements, be sure to disclose any information users might find dubious. For example, if you are reviewing a laptop computer on your blog and this laptop was provided by a manufacturer for the review, you should disclose that it was given to you by the manufacturer for the purpose of the review. If you do not share this critical piece of information, your users may view you and your methods as suspect. This goes straight to credibility and trust, and you should ensure that you do nothing to damage these things with your users. No matter how small or trivial, you should include information that will help your users see the entire picture. How you manage transparency can make the difference between success or failure for your blog.

■ ■ ■ ONLINE RESOURCE ■ ■ ■

The Federal Trade Commission recently put out documentation about how you need to manage testimonials and endorsements:

www.ftc.gov/opa/2009/10/endortest.shtm

The bottom line here is: you must be transparent now, or face the consequences.

■ ■ ■ Communities

Online communities exist for almost every topic imaginable. If you can think of a topic, in all likelihood you will find an online community discussing the topic in detail. Communities, also known as "forums" and "discussion boards," are excellent places to meet potential clients and expose them to your products and services. Please be certain, however, to understand the rules of engagement. Each community will have posted specific rules on how to interact with its users. By following these rules, you will be seen as a welcome contributing member of the community and encouraged to participate. If you stray outside of the rules, you will usually receive a warning from an owner or moderator, and if you continue to stay outside the bounds, you'll be asked to leave, or your account will simply be shut down.

Chances are that if you operate a Web site and your goal is either to sell a service or product, or even just to generate page views to showcase advertisements, participating in a community can be a worthwhile and rewarding experience, and also a lot of fun. By finding communities that are directly related to your Web site's topic, you can engage people who are prescreened and looking specifically for the information you're offering. By participating in these communities, you can learn a great deal, such as understanding which of your competitors does a good job of interacting with users, what types of information users are looking for on a given topic, what motivates users to take action, and what puts them off.

Most online communities take the form of running conversations. One user will start a topic, and other users will join the conversation, adding their own commentary. This is where your opportunity comes in to engage socially with this group. Since most discussion forums and communities are open for anyone to join, you can simply create an account and start participating. If your goal is to drive users to your own Web site, then take care to engage in thoughtful conversations and ensure that you bring meaningful contributions to each one. Everything you say will be a reflection on your Web site when users visit it. As in life, some people will generally agree with your point of view, while others will not. Just be sure to keep a civil tongue while participating in conversations and you'll be fine.

The software that enables these community forums to run long-form conversations usually allows users to create signatures, which will be appended to the comments or posts they make. This is an excellent location to include a link to your Web site or showcase information about your products or services. Please read the communities' rules about how you use the signature area, however. Some discussion areas forbid including links to your own Web site in your signature, and they many ban outright sales messages.

If you are unsure or the information is unclear, it's always best to ask outright what the rules are when you first introduce yourself. By doing so, you mark yourself as a law-abiding citizen within the group. And that first opportunity to introduce yourself should be taken with great care. This is an excellent opportunity to let users in this group know that you offer a related product or service, or that you have a Web site on a common topic that they may be interested in. It means you can usually post a link to your own Web site, by way of introduction, to show that you can contribute thoughtfully to the community. Make sure, however, to read any posted rules about what a forum administrator allows or disallows. After all, you want your first post to be positive.

Converting from a Community

Participating thoughtfully when you initially enter a community is the single best way to generate conversions. It does not matter whether you're selling a service, your own products, or showing ads on your Web site. By participating and growing your presence within the community as a respected member, users will be much more likely to frequent your Web site. I cannot stress enough the importance of being a regular contributing member to the community. Most online communities have a long memory and a short fuse. If you come in and sell, sell, sell right up front, you will often be shunned. If, however, you prove that you want to contribute in a meaningful way, the group will get to know you and see you as a resource.

An excellent way to grow credibility and enhance conversions is by bringing more value to the community through sharing information relevant to the topic, information that you either have gathered on your own or that you found. Users enjoy online communities as a way to learn and communicate information. If you are in a position to consistently bring useful information to community members, your expertise will be assured and you will reap benefits. If you can, include links back to your own Web site or services in your signature, for your signature can generate a tremendous amount of traffic and afford some visibility to the search engines. Get creative with your signature; you can often include images and multiple links, and you can select various fonts and colors. Individual forum rules will dictate what you can and cannot do. Once you know what is possible, make every effort to ensure that your signature includes clear sales messages, looks professional, and makes it easy for users to find the information they want.

If you can put multiple links in your signature, do so. Drop a link to each of the main areas of your Web site, enabling users to click on anything that catches their eye quickly and easily. Don't simply insert one link to your main page and hope users will find information from there. Take the time to break out the main areas of your Web site into individual links for placement in your signature. These main areas may include contact information, the section describing your products or services, and testimonials. You can use whatever you feel will best guide users to the relevant areas of your Web site provided that you follow the community's rules.

Converting from Your Own Community

Now, if you operate a discussion forum and your goal is to monetize your advertising, you may be thinking that this is an insurmountable task. While it will include editing your forum code to insert ads in select locations, this is generally pretty simple and can be completed with people possessing even a modest amount of HTML knowledge. Once again we can turn to Google for suggestions on how to best place ads within a community to generate clicks (Figure 9.2).

As in previous images, the darker an area, the better it is in generating clicks on advertisements. It may take some time to edit your code in order to achieve the best ad placement, but the time is well spent, for it will result in increased clicks and conversions. You can actually go a step further by including advertisements within the posts themselves. The goal should be to place your ads directly in the line of sight of readers without interrupting their search for information. This is a balancing act, but when you do it correctly, you can generate many clicks and more revenue.

You may also choose to add individual Web pages to a discussion forum to house static information that is commonly looked for by the group. These pages can be built and set up in any format you choose, which affords you an opportu-

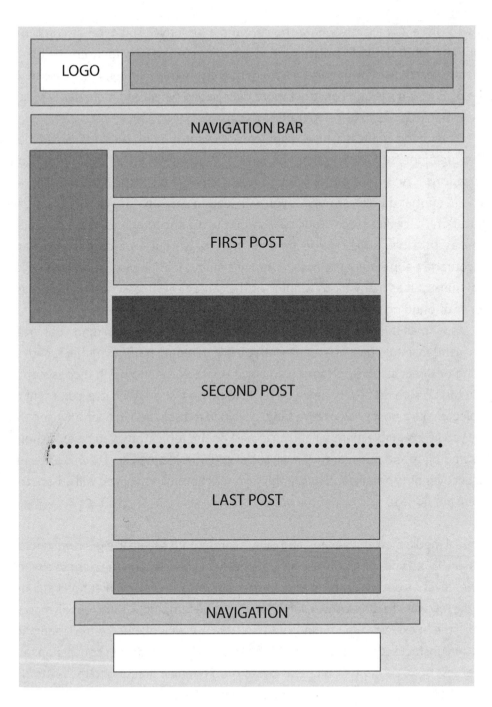

Figure 9.2. Google suggestions for ads in a blog

nity to place ads exactly where they are most effective. This type of combined approach lends depth to a discussion forum and makes it easy for users to find frequently searched information. By adding content in this manner, you increase the size of the Web site and construct more Web pages, which can more easily rank in the search engines to develop traffic for you.

Developing traffic is critical. People don't want to hang out in an area where they are alone, so ensuring that you have a steady flow of traffic and good conversations is an important task when maintaining a discussion forum. This will require effort if the site is yours, as you will need to participate in almost every conversation that takes place. Your goal should be to encourage as much conversation as possible, so set aside time to start new topics of conversation and encourage people to participate. If you are maintaining a discussion forum, you can think of it as many blogs running at the same time. In essence, the forum is a series of ongoing conversations.

As with all things social, the main theme is credibility. By building your credibility and maintaining it at a high level, you will generate traffic, whether for advertising or direct sales. By choosing an appropriate voice and using it consistently, you can be sure that every time you participate on a social Web site, comment on a blog, make a post on your own blog, or join in a discussion in a forum, users will see you as a valuable member and an expert on the topic. Your watchwords should be credibility and transparency in all social activities. Some users seem to live just to uncover dirty details, and by planning your actions carefully you will ensure that there are none to uncover about you.

If social media marketing, blogs, and online communities seem like great ways to get personal with your potential users, in the next chapter I'll open the door to a whole other level of personalization and conversion rates: e-mail marketing is still one of the top ways to drive conversions. You might be tempted to lump e-mail marketing in the bucket with spamming, but think twice. A well-planned e-mail marketing campaign, focused on a select, well-defined e-mail list can deliver conversion rates in excess of 80 percent. Don't be so fast to drop e-mail marketing to the bottom of the pile, because getting it right can make you a hero.

10

E-mail Marketing: Tread Carefully to Reap Great Rewards

BEFORE GETTING INTO the tips and tricks of e-mail marketing, it is important to cover some basic details. There are rules to follow—rules that if broken can result in legal ramifications—so pay attention and plan your program carefully. It's easy to stay inside the limits, but setting your expectations unrealistically high could quickly lead you astray.

E-mail marketing is a highly personal way to reach your users, much more personal than even social media marketing. As such, you must carefully craft your messages—sales pitches, informational updates, subscription requests, and so on—and plan who will receive which ones. Don't assume a blanket message will work overall. E-mail marketing will test your ability to think in terms of niches by encouraging you to segment your e-mail list based on reader responses. Truly, if you plan your e-mail program and campaigns with care, you'll find success. It may take years for you to develop a solid internal e-mailing list, but the effort is well worth it, as your ability to generate conversions, practically "on command," will be impressive.

What You Need to Know First

E-mail remains one of the single best ways to develop conversions. Many businesses see conversion rates in excess of 80 percent from e-mails they send to their internal mailing lists. While everyone is familiar with spam, as we all receive it every day, it's important to know the distinction between spam and legitimate e-mail marketing. You may be aware of the CAN-SPAM legislation, enacted in December 2003, but it's important that you learn the details of how to comply with the law before operating your own e-mail marketing campaigns. The CAN-SPAM legislation places the burden on you to maintain an e-mailing program within the law. Become familiar with this legislation and the main points of compliance before you start your own e-mail program. The following information, which comes direct from the Federal Trade Commission's Web site, offers a rundown on the main points of the legislation.

1. **Don't use false or misleading header information.** All routing information—the From, To, Reply-To, originating domain name, and e-mail address—must be accurate and identify the person or business that initiated the message.
2. **Don't use deceptive subject lines.** The subject line must accurately reflect the content of the message. Using a subject line mentioning the latest movie in a series and then showing content in the e-mail selling only the older versions of the movie would be seen as deceptive. We'll discuss the subject line more fully later.
3. **Identify the message as an ad.** The law gives you a lot of leeway in how to do this, but you must disclose clearly and conspicuously that your message is an advertisement.
4. **Tell recipients where you're located.** Your message must include your valid physical postal address. This can be your current street address, a post office box you've registered with the U.S. Postal Service, or a private mailbox you've registered with a commercial mail receiving agency established under Postal Service regulations.

5. **Tell recipients how to opt out of receiving future e-mail from you.** Your message must include a clear and conspicuous explanation of how the recipient can opt out of getting e-mail from you in the future. The notice must be crafted in a way that's easy for an ordinary person to recognize, read, and understand. Creative use of type size, color, and location can improve clarity. You must include a return e-mail address or another Internet-based way to allow people to communicate their choices to you. You may create a menu option that allows recipients to opt out of certain types of messages, but you must include the option to stop all commercial messages from you. Make sure your spam filter doesn't block these opt-out requests.

6. **Honor opt-out requests promptly.** A recipient's opt-out request must be honored within 10 business days, and whichever opt-out mechanism you have in place must be capable of processing opt-out requests for at least 30 days after you send your message. E-mail marketers cannot charge a fee, ask the recipient to reveal any personally identifying information beyond an e-mail address, or require any step other than sending a reply e-mail or visiting a single page on a Web site as a condition for honoring an opt-out request. Once people have said they don't want to receive more messages, you can't sell or transfer their e-mail addresses, even in the form of a mailing list. The only exception is that you may transfer the addresses to a company you've hired to help you comply with the CAN-SPAM Act.

7. **Monitor what others are doing on your behalf.** The law makes clear that even if you hire another company to handle your e-mail marketing, you can't contract away your legal responsibility to comply with the law. Both the company whose product is promoted in the message and the company that actually sends the message may be held legally responsible for any infraction.

This information and much more can be located on the FTC Web site: www.ftc.gov/bcp/edu/pubs/business/ecommerce/bus61.shtm. With fines ranging up to $16,000 for *each* infraction (each e-mail sent outside compliance), violating this law can be costly.

Now, don't let all the regulatory and compliance issues frighten you, as e-mail marketing remains one of the top forms of marketing online today in terms of conversions. The ability to reach out directly and have one-on-one conversations with individuals is an unparalleled opportunity to support a selling message. At some point users have expressed interest in hearing from you by giving you their e-mail addresses. This permission allows you to feed select pieces of information directly to users to influence their behavior. And while this tacit permission exists, you should not push the limits. How you set up and run your e-mail program will help determine how successful it is at developing conversions.

■ ■ ■ Getting Started: It's All About the E-mail List

A well-run e-mail marketing program will be based on an internally developed e-mail list. By capturing this data at point of sale or through sign-up forms on your own Web site, you are growing an in-house list of people who are already interested in doing business with you. This type of list is the best, for it converts well. You should not purchase a list and simply begin sending e-mails to the addresses on it, though. Most spam comes from lists such as these. By developing your own list, you overcome the hurdles surrounding permission-based marketing.

The biggest hurdle you will encounter is actually obtaining users' permission to contact them. Most e-mail systems today are end-to-end systems, meaning they capture e-mail on the front end and follow up with users to assure that confirmation action is taken. This confirmation usually comes in the form of an e-mail that requires users to click on a link that your business sends to them. By clicking the link, users confirm permission for you to send e-mails to them. Most e-mail software systems or companies providing e-mailing services can manage this entire cycle for your business, if this is how you wish to build an e-mail list. If you already have a lot of traffic on your Web site, using such systems is an excellent way to begin capturing and growing your own internal e-mail list, whether through stand-alone software or through a service provided by a third party.

Users expect you to deliver relevant and timely information. For this reason, it is important that you plan your e-mail program carefully. By ensuring communication on a regular basis, your users will know when they can expect to hear from you. In this way you can train users to watch for your communication. If users perceive that you deliver value, they will wait with anticipation for your next message.

If you have a small e-mail list, you can contact those on it via normal e-mail programs, such as Microsoft Outlook or Google's Gmail. You should be careful about running up against limits imposed by your e-mail service provider, but, generally, sending e-mails to hundreds of people is doable. As your list grows and you start to send to thousands of people, you should consider a stand-alone service, whether it is software you install and manage yourself or, as is increasingly popular, contracting a third-party company to handle this process on your behalf. Here are a few firms that offer this service:

Constant Contact
www.constantcontact.com
iContact
www.icontact.com
Emma
www.myemma.com

Many medium- and large-scale businesses would do best to use third parties to manage their e-mail campaigns. These third-party systems are designed to manage large volumes and to comply with legislation. They usually offer a vast array of options to help you customize and personalize the e-mails sent to people on your list. They also offer the service of managing the list, meaning they take care of ensuring that new e-mail addresses are captured and old ones removed. If an e-mail bounces, they will scrub it from the list; and if a user chooses to be removed, they will manage this as well. These systems also usually come with a vast array of tracking already in place.

Tracking your e-mails and how users interact with them is critical to running a successful e-mail marketing campaign. Each component included in your e-mail needs to be tracked individually: every offer, every image, every link. You need to understand how the vast majority of recipients are interacting with this communication if you want to refine it and increase conversions. Most systems are advanced enough to capture click-through rates across each and every component of an e-mail. Some are even capable of tracking when users hover over potential links but do not click through. This information is vital to help you fine-tune your sales message. By looking through this information and strategically modifying the e-mail itself, you can help increase the click-through rate and drive more users to your Web site.

■ ■ ■ How to Get Conversions

Converting from clean, self-built e-mail lists is one of the easier methods of driving sales. Think about it: if users enjoyed the experience they first had with you enough to leave their e-mail addresses, they will likely visit you again when you e-mail them. If users made purchases from you in the past and you captured their e-mail through this process, even better—they've already proven their willingness to purchase from you, so most of your work is done.

Let's discuss getting conversions under the premise that you are building your own internal e-mail list as opposed to purchasing one.

While purchasing a list may seem like a faster way to reach out to a large number of people, the inherent problem is that you have no way to verify the quality of the list you are purchasing. Often, list-sellers will allow you to buy a portion of the list, which includes legitimate e-mails. Upon seeing positive results for this test group, you agree to purchase the entire list. It is only after you've gotten to this point, when you begin sending out tens of thousands or even millions of e-mails, that you realize the rest of the list is essentially garbage.

When you build your own list internally, each person added to it has been pre-qualified and has made the decision to opt in to hear from you again. Whether you build this list via an e-mail capture form on your Web pages or you collect the e-mails only when you complete sales, this type of list is always a better place to start your e-mail campaigns. While it may take longer for you to develop a deep list, it is well worth the wait, because the quality of this list will be far higher than any list you can purchase today.

The first step in ensuring conversions from your e-mail list is making sure the list is clean and current. This is why, as mentioned before, you should look at e-mail systems that automatically manage subscription requests and "unsubscribes" from your users. If your e-mail system manages this for you, your list will always be current and ready for use. It will also help ensure your compliance with regulations. Just having a good e-mail list does not guarantee conversions, though. While it is the first step, what you do to segment this list will have a more profound effect on your conversion rate success. By carefully tracking the results of each e-mailing and the sales that follow, you will begin to see patterns emerge among the e-mails contained within your list. Use these patterns to help you understand how to segment the list. Some users will be lured back with deep discounts. Others will respond to the fact that you're offering them early access to a sale, while still others may need to wait or will respond simply because they recognize your e-mail and business name.

One of your goals during the refining process is to break your large list into smaller lists. Each of these smaller lists will then get tested to understand which offers and incentives encourage more visits and higher conversions. There are endless ways to segment an e-mail list, so you should be watching your results to determine how to create these smaller, more targeted lists. If you think of your larger e-mail list as a stadium full of people, it's easier to understand how different groups of people will be moved by common interests. Some simply want to watch the game. Others are diehard fans wearing body paint instead of shirts. Approaching each takes a different path, as they respond to different things. If you want to engage these different groups, the best way is to understand what moves each group and to cater to that need or desire. The goal of segmenting your larger list is to define these different groups, with an eye toward encouraging users within a specific segment of your list to respond.

The next step, even within the smaller grouping, is to extend multiple versions of the same e-mail to test for finer variations, which can impact conversion rates.

Pay close attention to where you place your images, where you place your call to action, and how much text you have overall in your e-mail. You may find, for example, that text-only e-mails bring in a higher response rate, and thus higher conversions, than image-heavy versions. This could be due to e-mail settings and user accounts that are set to block images, thus leaving an image-heavy e-mail in which the images appear fragmented or blank. The opposite may also apply, wherein you have fewer responses but higher conversion rates from e-mails rich in imagery and that showcase products directly to users. While there is little you can do about users' settings, you can explain in your e-mail how to best access communication from your business. It is perfectly acceptable to suggest that users turn on all images for the optimal experience. These small things can have a profound impact on your ability to increase conversions from your e-mail lists.

■ ■ ■ Refining E-mails

Other areas in e-mail marketing that need your attention are your subject line, your salutation, your body copy, and your sign-off.

Subject Line

This is the very first thing users encounter when they receive your e-mail, so it is critical that your subject line performs its job flawlessly each and every time. Its one and only goal is to get users to open the e-mail, thus exposing them to the real message.

Your subject line should be clear, concise, and factual. You also need to use select and targeted keywords with the goal of getting users to open the e-mail. You should be relentless in testing your subject lines and looking carefully through your statistics to understand which versions performed the best. By testing variations of your subject line against small portions of a list, you'll be better positioned to know which version of the subject line to use more broadly. If subject line A tests at a 3 percent open rate and subject line B tests at a 6 percent open rate, it's obvious you should be using subject line B for your mass mailing. Performing simple tasks like this on small segments of the mailing list is an excellent way to increase your conversion rates.

Salutation

The salutation is your chance to connect personally with your e-mail recipients. If you have captured users' first names, you should be using them in your salutation. Personalized e-mails enjoy a higher response rate, click-through rate, and conversion rate than anonymous e-mails. Another reason to test your system is that often, when users sign up for your e-mail list on your Web site and enter their first and last names, the e-mail system may blend these together in the salutation line. To users this seems awkward and obviously generated by machine. Your goal should be to have each e-mail appear as if it were coming directly from you and going to nobody except the recipient.

Body Copy

The body copy of your e-mail contains the critical information you're trying to get in front of your users. If the subject line has done its job, users will now be staring directly at your body copy. You have precious little time, often just seconds, to engage users directly. Maximize this time by creating body copy that showcases clearly your main message and displays prominently a call to action. It is important that readers know as quickly as possible exactly what you want them to do. While you can use long form, paragraph-style writing to convey your message, in most cases short, simple, bulleted lists work much better at guiding readers in the direction you want them to go.

Around your body copy, don't be afraid to include things such as testimonials from others who have taken action and have used your products or services. By providing extra information, you give users a frame of reference to understand that others have successfully done business with you or taken the same action and been happy with the results. You should take care, however, to ensure that this extra information does not detract from the original message or distract users. Often it is the simplest messages that generate the highest click-through and conversion rates.

If you've done your job segmenting your list, you will know which offers and incentives motivate each group. You can use this knowledge to craft body copy specifically for each group. This approach has the highest percentage of success in increasing click-throughs and conversions.

Sign-Off

As you sign off on your e-mail, take the opportunity to remind users of time limits on any of your offers or of any other specific information that is critical for them to understand. You should also use this sign-off to cement your personal relationship with each recipient. By signing an actual name to every e-mail, users feel there is a direct communication between someone at your business and themselves. This is a small but significant detail, and it relies heavily on relationship psychology to influence further communications and responses.

If you take the time to follow these steps, you will know how to segment your larger e-mail list, and you'll clearly understand the subtle nuances that affect which offers, verbiage, and incentives elicit the desired response from each smaller group within that list. E-mail marketing can be one of the most successful ways of generating repeat conversions. It is particularly useful for Web sites that showcase and sell products. Take care to follow the rules and build meaningful e-mail relationships with those on your list. In doing so, you will enjoy repeat customers who are as happy to do business with you as you are with them.

Even with the power of e-mail to drive big conversion rates, you need to keep in mind that without a well-conceived checkout system, all your efforts may be for naught. While the section on checkouts in the next chapter will apply only to some readers, it's worth reading to gain more insight into the things that can influence buyer decisions. It will reveal all the details for optimizing and refining the shopping cart process, with an eye toward capturing more of the lost conversions from users who simply abandon their carts. As you'll see, even the smallest changes can yield large results.

11

Shopping Carts: Optimizing the Checkout Process

IF YOU RUN AN e-commerce style Web site or sell directly from your Web site, optimizing your shopping cart is a critical step. All of your other efforts can be undone if your shopping cart encourages users to quit their session prematurely. While shopping carts are complex pieces of code, their complexity shouldn't impact the user's experience in a negative way. In fact, the user experience should be simple and seamless from start to finish.

While there are many schools of thought on exactly how to manage the checkout process, one mode rarely fails in the end: short, simple, and sweet. Lately, more and more, Web sites will allow you to check out as a guest without having to open an account or join in any way. While they still require your name, address, phone number, and billing information, many Web sites give you the option of dispensing with the hassle of joining and managing future correspondence. They very clearly explain this and permit you to decide for yourself.

Whether you choose to start your checkout process in this manner is entirely up to you, but think carefully about whether your users are onetime purchasers or if you cater to a crowd that you expect to come back repeatedly. While ultimately you should have a goal of creating return visits and return shopping experiences, in some cases this simply won't happen. Allowing users a choice is an excellent way to indicate to them that you value their privacy.

Choose your checkout software very carefully. Always insist on a full run-through, and test the system for your users prior to going live. It is critical that the system work flawlessly each and every time for each and every user. If your users are guinea pigs in sorting out the bugs and problems of a new system, they will quickly tire of this and shop elsewhere.

Most off-the-shelf systems today are relatively well put together and offer a decent checkout experience. For larger Web sites, there is often a need to customize these systems. But do not let the need for customization interfere with a smooth checkout process for users. If at any point you have to ask yourself whether to make this trade-off and have users complete another step, the answer is: make the trade. Never make users take another action.

Your checkout process should be visually clean and simple. At this point in the cycle, users are about to exchange cash for a product they have not yet physically held and for which they will have to wait. It is very important that they have a sense of being expertly taken care of at your Web site. If users get distracted and confused by a visually complicated process, in many cases they will simply end the session and shop elsewhere. Then, in addition to losing the direct sale, there is a ripple effect in which users now have a negative association with your Web site.

It is exponentially harder to encourage users to come back after a negative experience, and much more cost effective to generate repeat sales from the same customers than to attract new ones. So you should be sure that every experience users have with you is positive and that you keep them as long-term clients. Therefore, make every effort to streamline your checkout process so that the moment users part with their hard-earned cash, they feel that you are a partner in providing them with what they want. If instead they feel they need to fight with you along the way, or that you make it difficult for them to give you their money, they will turn to another source.

While each situation will be unique, there are common areas that everyone needs to manage. Because of this overlap, it is highly recommended that you either partner with a company that specializes in managing a checkout process or, at the very least, that you purchase software and have it professionally installed. For one thing, your system will need to process credit cards, which means that, as with any other business, you'll need to be vetted by the credit card companies. By partnering with a company that already provides the service and using its checkout process, you can easily manage this step and get set up quickly. Of course, no matter how highly recommended a company is, insist on being able to walk through the purchase process on a live Web site with a current client. Reputable companies will have no problem honoring this request, and you'll get a firsthand look at what your user experience will be like. Services like this do cost money, so be prepared to do your research and budget it as a monthly expense.

If at any step in the checkout process you encounter an issue or something you think might be a problem, call it out and ask if it can be customized or smoothed for your users. Simple things can make all the difference, such as a small check box allowing users to quickly copy their shipping information as their billing information. By enabling this one check box, you save users many minutes. In addition, you've created goodwill toward your Web site, which validates the feelings of trust and encourages users to do business with you in the future. While much of this is psychological, much of the sales process as a whole is psychological. The net result for enabling a small check box could be thousands of sales a month or year to your Web site.

Part of managing the user checkout and shopping experience is ensuring that users can quickly locate and identify a link to their current shopping carts. A standard location seems to be in the top right-hand area of most e-commerce Web sites. The goal here is to allow users quick access to view the items they have placed in their carts. Some Web sites, notably Amazon.com, capture users once they're engaged in the shopping cart experience. While they encourage users to add other related items, they don't make it easy for them to go back to the main Web site to search for more things. Given that it's Amazon, which does relentless testing, I'm sure they have a very good reason for doing this.

Don't assume, however, that just because a large Web site does something, you should do it too. You are not Amazon, after all. You should spend time in your research phase viewing the checkout process of many large Web sites. The upside is that you get to enjoy some retail therapy while learning what a good checkout process looks like.

■ ■ ■ Several Checkout Processes

Some Web sites seem to have been designed with the idea that by adding as many items as possible into the checkout chain they will increase sales. In some cases this approach does actually work, though usually it results in confusion. By preselecting and adding certain things, and simply showing a user an end result and dollar amount, sales are increased directly. This is not a positive user experience and usually does not result in return visits. This is very much a case of short-term gain at the expense of long-term success. Web sites practicing these tactics often develop a reputation for poor customer service. In fact, many mainstream retail e-commerce Web sites do not do this. Let's take a look at a couple of examples of different systems and how they compare.

Example 1: GoDaddy.com

GoDaddy.com is a great site for purchasing domains and for hosting Web sites. Despite having some difficulties with its customer service team, most customers find the site reliable. When purchasing several items, customers end up with decent discounts, and periodically account holders with more Web sites receive additional discounts. Unfortunately, GoDaddy has an overly complicated checkout process. Let's walk through the process for a domain purchase, and then you can draw your own conclusions.

Step 1. Select the Domain You Want

On this first page in Figure 11.1, you will notice a couple of different things. First is a long list of alternate domain names related to the one you chose. This list is a quick way for you to understand the other top level domains that are available. In this case you were apparently going after a very specific .com domain name. You will note about midway through the image (in the small section below the larger list of domains) an area where two versions of the domain name appear. The first item is the actual domain you were looking for (scripttag.com), while the second was a typo that was made intentionally (scriptag.com). Both of these are selected automatically for you. This automatic selection carries over to the shopping cart later in the process.

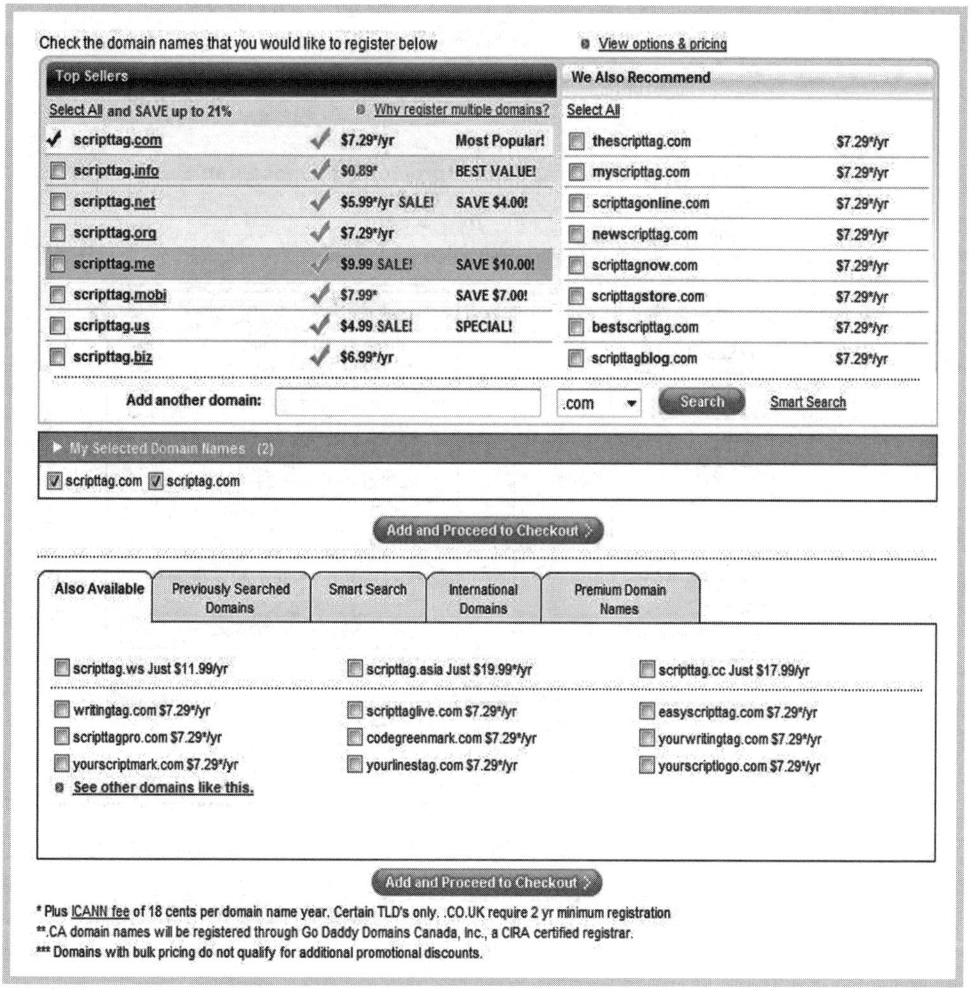

Figure 11.1. Domain selection screen

Step 2. Stopped for Offers

When you click on the "Add and Proceed to Checkout" button (Figure 11.1), an intermediary page pops up (Figure 11.2). The point behind this page is to alert you to other opportunities while your buying temperature is still high. The "Add to Cart" buttons are featured prominently, while the button you would click to skip this opportunity ("No Thanks") is featured less prominently. While this book shows the examples in shades of gray, the actual Web site shows them with the "Add and Proceed to Checkout" button in bright orange and the "No Thanks" button in dull gray.

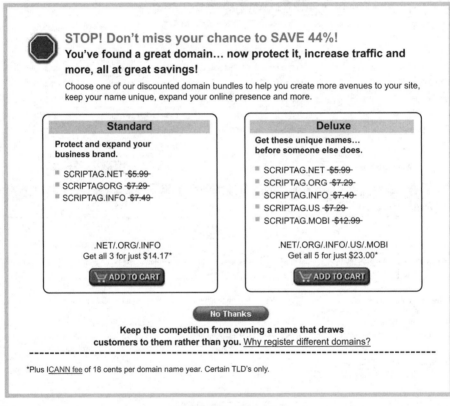

Figure 11.2. Offer

Step 3. Registration and Checkout Options

On this page (Figure 11.3), you will notice that in the area labeled "Your Domain Names," the number 2 is in parentheses. This number represents both the original domain you wanted plus the typo (scriptag.com). In order for you to notice that you made a typo at this point, you'd have to click on the small plus symbol (+) next to the text "Domains on this order." Doing so will showcase each of the domains in the list. Also worth noting is the fact that the two-year option is automatically selected for you in the registration length column, effectively doubling your cost and the length of ownership, since your original intention was to purchase the domain for one year.

After clicking the "Continue" button (not shown in Figure 11.3), you end up on the page in Figure 11.4 (which happens to have a similar "Continue" button as on the

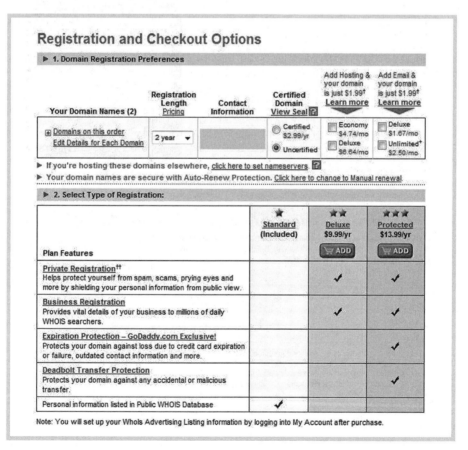

Figure 11.3. Registration and checkout options

last page), containing information about setting up your Web site immediately or moving to the final phase of the checkout process. In the image, in the circular options button under "4. Select Checkout Preference," "SHOW ME great deals on hosting . . . ," the first two words are in all caps and the whole line is in boldface type. In this default setting, if you click the "Continue" button, you'll be shown more options, all of which are available for purchase. You must select: "No thanks . . ." before going forward, otherwise you'll be pulled even further away from checking out. Keep that "default setting" ploy in mind as you scroll through the rest of the process.

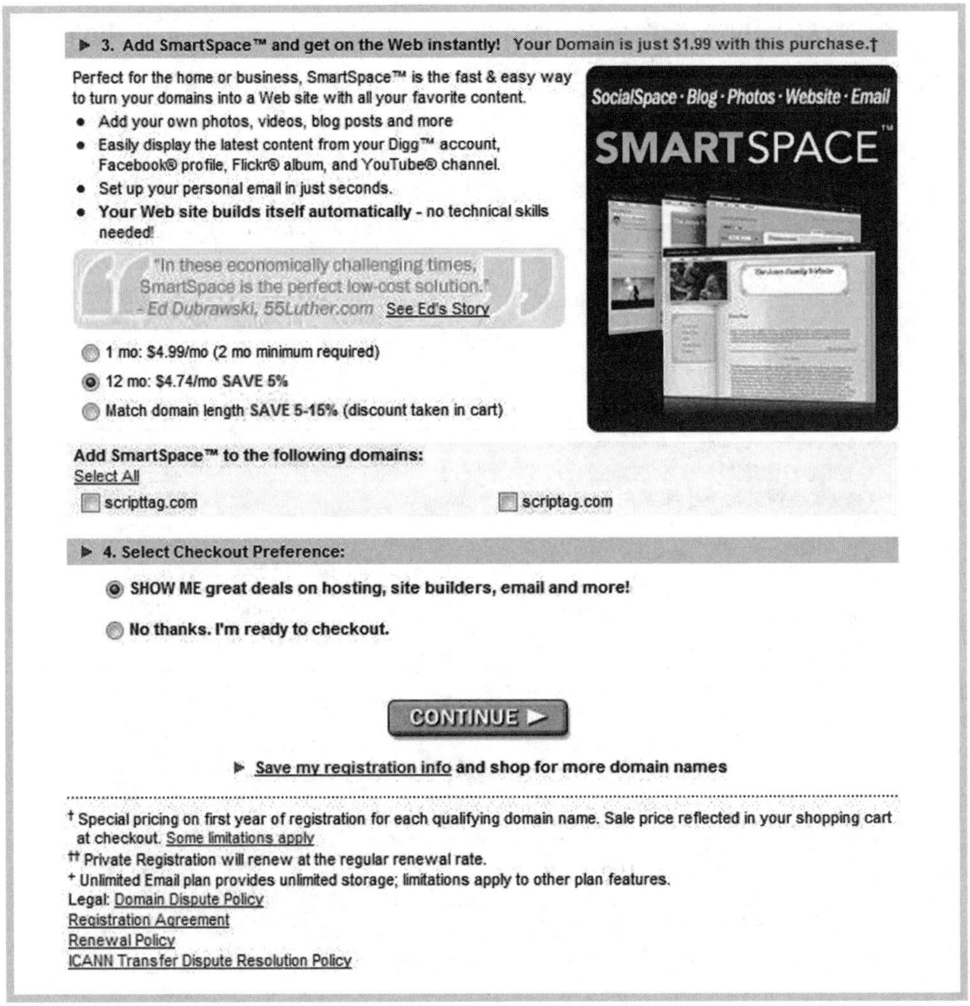

Figure 11.4. More options

Step 4. Reviewing Your Order

At this stage you would have removed the extra domain and also selected the domain registration as one year instead of the default option of two years. Doing so has allowed you to capture the actual price, as you can see in Figure 11.5. From this point on the checkout procedure is straightforward and simple.

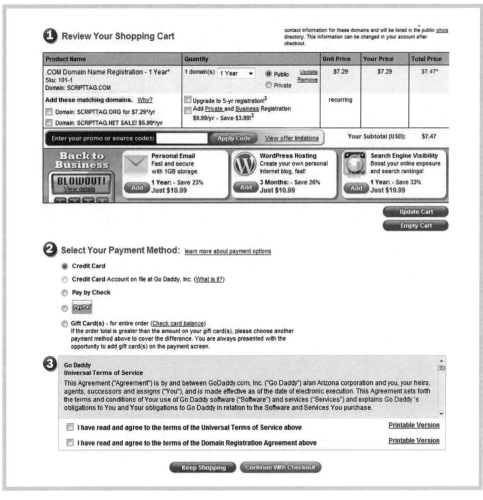

Figure 11.5. Reviewing the order

Step 5. Billing Information

Figure 11.6 shows where you add your name, mailing address, e-mail address, work phone, credit card information. It also shows where to click to place your order.

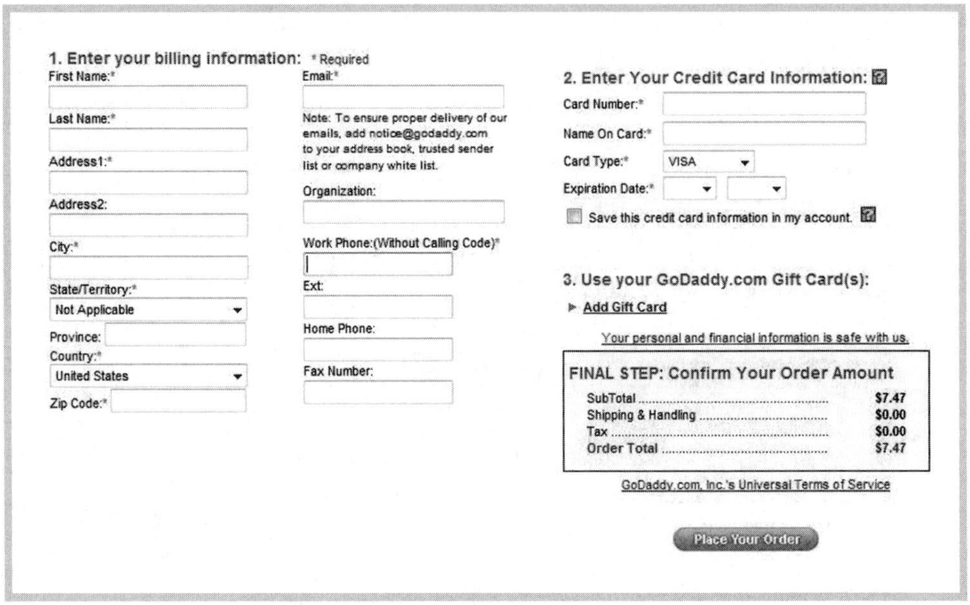

Figure 11.6. Billing information

Step 6. Verifying Page

In Figure 11.7, you are called upon to verify the access code.

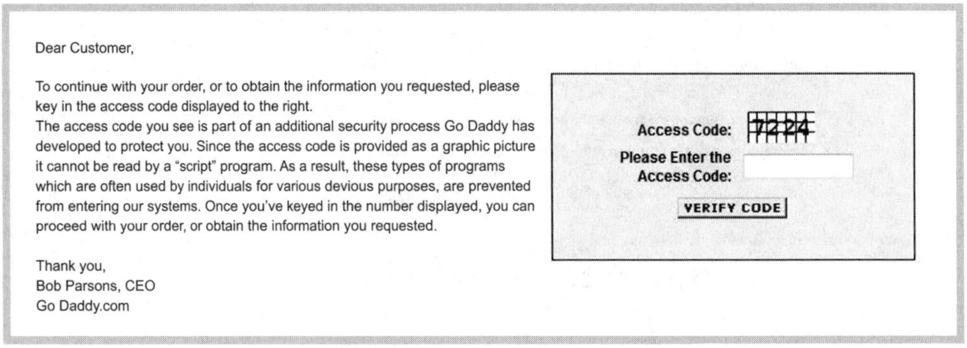

Figure 11.7. Verify code

Step 7. Thank-You Page and Final Offers

Figure 11.8 showcases an often overlooked opportunity to increase conversions: using the confirmation page to suggest add-ons and extra purchases. While much of the GoDaddy checkout process is overly complicated, this is one practice you would do well to emulate. This approach is similar to constructing a 404 error page that includes links to popular areas of your Web site with the goal of recapturing traffic that might otherwise leave (we're not covering custom 404 pages here, but a quick search for that phrase online will help you out). After users have purchased on your site, the time is ideal to showcase related products and services. It can be a very effective way to boost sales and increase conversions.

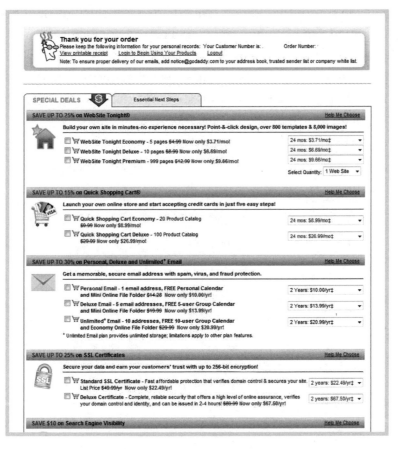

Figure 11.8. Final offers

Example 2: Amazon.com

Now let's look at our second example. We'll follow the steps and make a product purchase online.

Step 1. Inside the Cart, Items Ready to Go

The image in Figure 11.9 represents what happens after placing items in your shopping cart at Amazon.com. The next step is to decide your shipping preference. You're offered two choices: having as few shipments as possible or having items shipped as available, which means you would receive them faster. Faster in that Amazon will process shipping your items as each is available, rather than waiting for all items to become available and then shipping everything at that time. Following that, you can select a shipping speed. This order qualifies for the free shipping option, which is what you selected, but obviously you would pay a premium if you selected the overnight shipping option instead. Below, a clearly defined button allows you to change quantities of items purchased, or even delete them completely from the shopping cart. Finally, there is a line containing the shipping address (though the address cannot be seen in this figure) and then a list of the items.

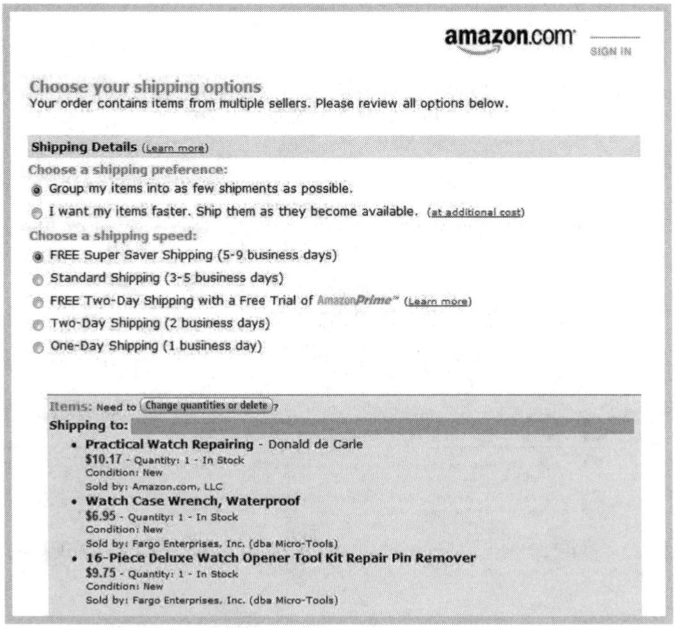

Figure 11.9. Shipping options

Step 2. Payment Information

The payment information screen in Figure 11.10 is a model of simplicity. All you do is enter your credit card information—your shipping information is captured already—and it will be added to the other information about your account. Now, Amazon has everything it needs to process an order. Also, at this stage you're given the opportunity to enter gift cards or promotional code information, to apply for and use an Amazon.com store credit card, or even to link information directly to your checking account. This is an excellent series of payment options to present to users.

In addition, if you look at the very top of Figure 11.10, there is a clear path that shows you your progress through the entire checkout process. In this case you are two steps in. Step 3 can be easily skipped if you're not interested in gift-wrapping. In effect, this means the checkout process that Amazon.com offers is three pages in depth: short and sweet.

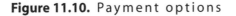

Figure 11.10. Payment options

Step 3. Enter Billing Address Information

Because this is your first time using this credit card with Amazon.com, you are shown an intermediary page (Figure 11.11) where you could link an address to the credit card information on file. This page is very clear, and there are no sales messages, as its goal is to simply allow you to enter your billing information.

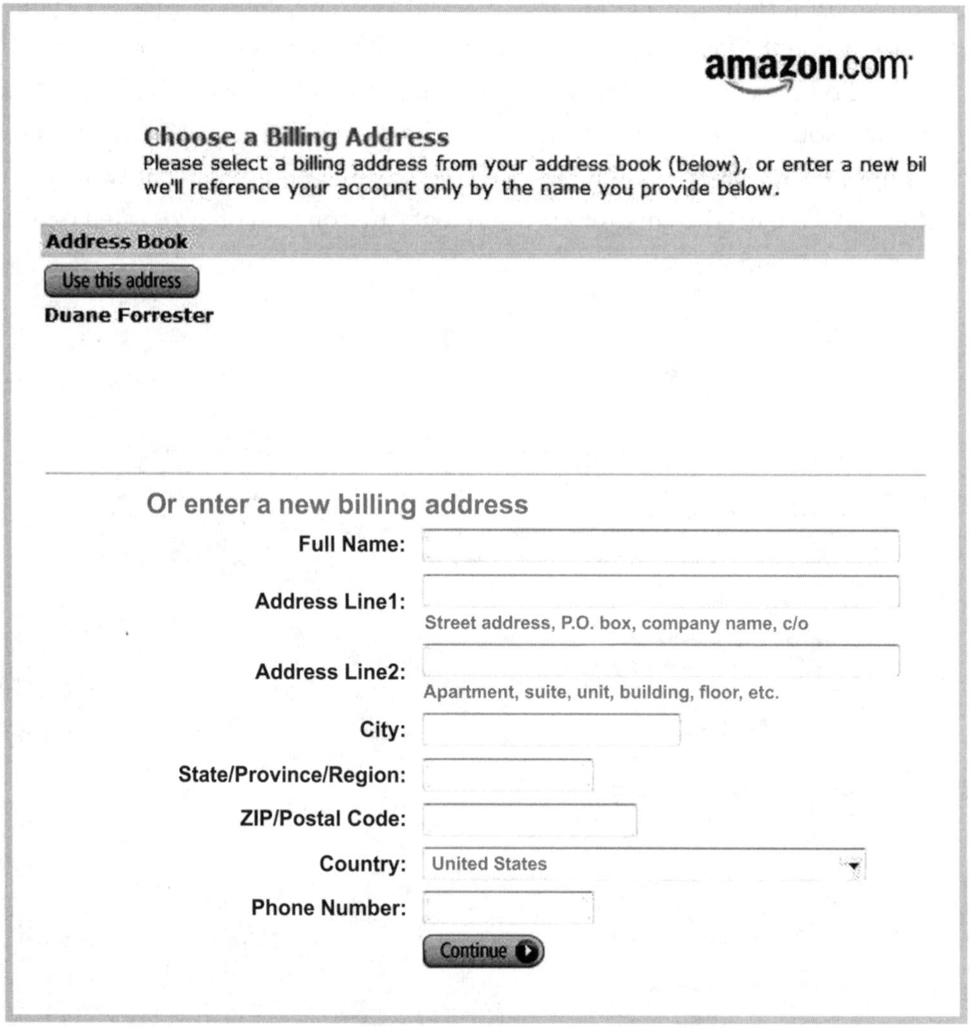

Figure 11.11. Billing information

Step 4. Confirm Your Order Information

The page shown in Figure 11.12 is an excellent overview of the entire purchase prior to selecting the "Place your order" button. Your name, address, and phone number are verified, as is your order, shipping, and billing information. You are given a final chance to change the order quantity and shipping method, and to use a gift card. This summary gives you all the information you need to ensure that the order is for the products you desire, and it gives you a clear cost breakdown. The only thing left to do at this point is to click "Submit" and complete the order.

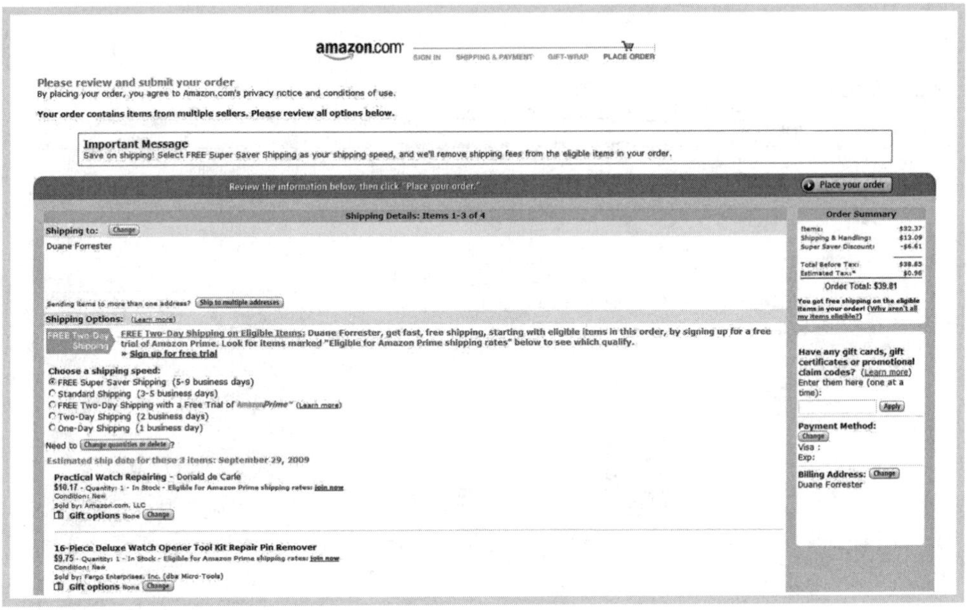

Figure 11.12. Confirmation

Step 5. Thank-You Page

The final page in the transaction process thanks you for placing your order (Figure 11.13). While a thank-you message may seem lost on this page with its numerous images, the area where this message is delineated, near the top, is clear enough. The message is short and to the point: you will receive an e-mail confirmation soon. That confirmation will contain a summary of the order, tracking information, and the expected delivery date.

This page is also designed to sell other items related to previous purchases. Apparently Amazon also thinks you might want to buy flowers . . .

Figure 11.13. Thank-you page

Example 3: BlueDial.com

While the previous two examples were from Web sites that are generally well-known, this next example is from a smaller, less mainstream Web site.

Step 1. Place Item in Cart

When you have narrowed down the product search, the next step on the page in Figure 11.14 is obvious. A prominent "Add to Cart" button clearly stands out, and a good deal of relevant information is also available, including the price; an "enlargeable" image of the product, and fine print displaying the information that BlueDial is an authorized dealer for this particular make and model of watch. This information is critical for ensuring that buyers have a sense of security while shopping on a Web site.

In the lower right-hand corner of the screen you'll see a logo that shows the site is bonded, meaning any purchase made through BlueDial will be covered for more than the value of the product. The company that backs the service has periodic ongoing testing, which ensures that if there are any problems, the vendor can fix them immediately.

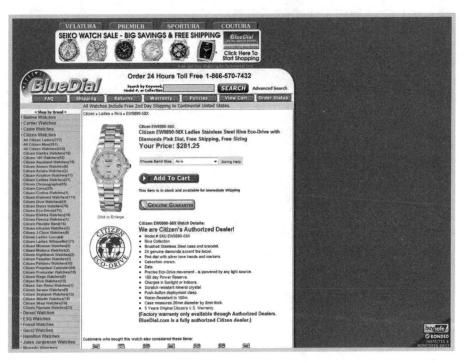

Figure 11.14. Adding to cart

Step 2. Order Confirmation

In Figure 11.15, the vendor offers a summary review of the product you're shopping for, information on the service for bonded coverage, shipping options, and a clear direction to proceed to get to checkout. In addition, this Web site takes the time to explain all of the various payment options, ensuring that however you choose to pay, you'll be securely covered. Finally, at the bottom of the page you'll find contact information, including an e-mail address (behind the clickable text seen as "Contact Us"), a postal address, a direct-dial telephone number, and hours of operation. The inclusion of a phone number tells you that if you have any questions, there will be an opportunity to actually speak to a person to move things forward. While the time may be limited to a very specific window, it is still more service than many online retailers offer their customers.

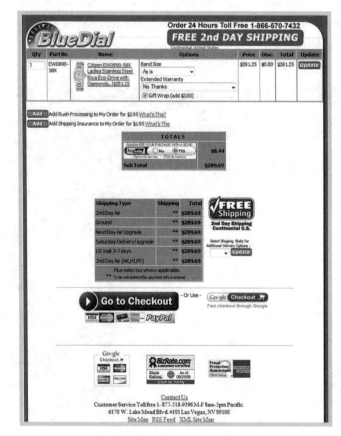

Figure 11.15. Order confirmation

Step 3. Shipping and Billing Information

While the page in Figure 11.16 may seem daunting, with all the blank forms, it takes very little time to complete. On one side you fill in your billing information, and on the other you simply click a small check box to indicate that your shipping information is the same as your billing information, which is then prepopulated for you. In the next section, farther down, you provide your credit card information, which is followed by an overview of the return policy through which you can scroll. Finally there's a large button to continue the checkout process.

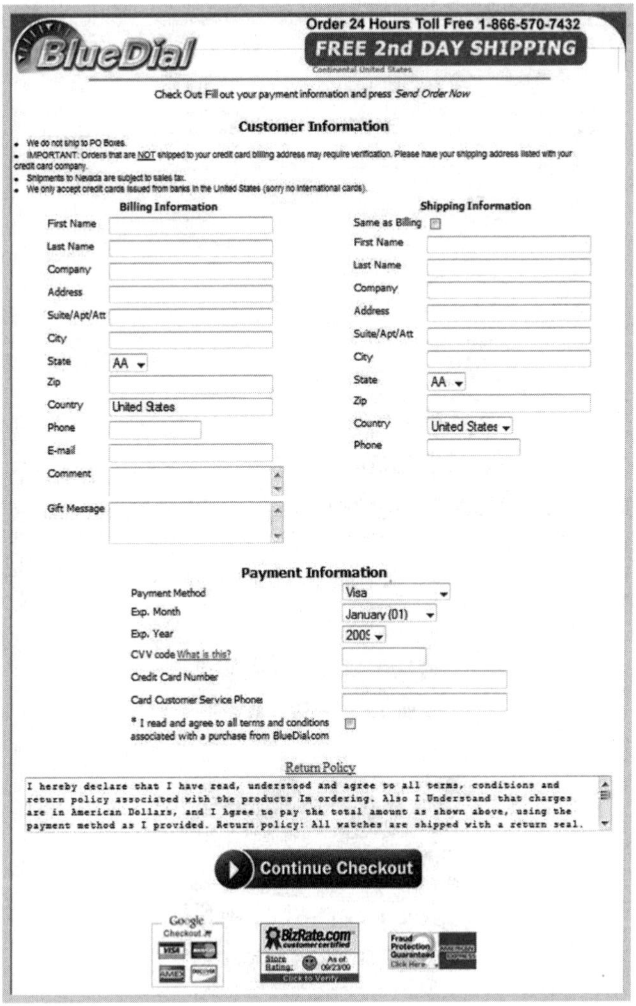

Figure 11.16. Shipping and billing

Step 4. Shipping and Billing Confirmation

Figure 11.17 presents an entire summary view of your billing, shipping, and product information, as well as the button needed to complete the order. You'll notice that none of these pages thus far contains any extraneous information, any extra advertising or other information or objects that would distract users from purchasing. The checkout process is extremely clean and straightforward.

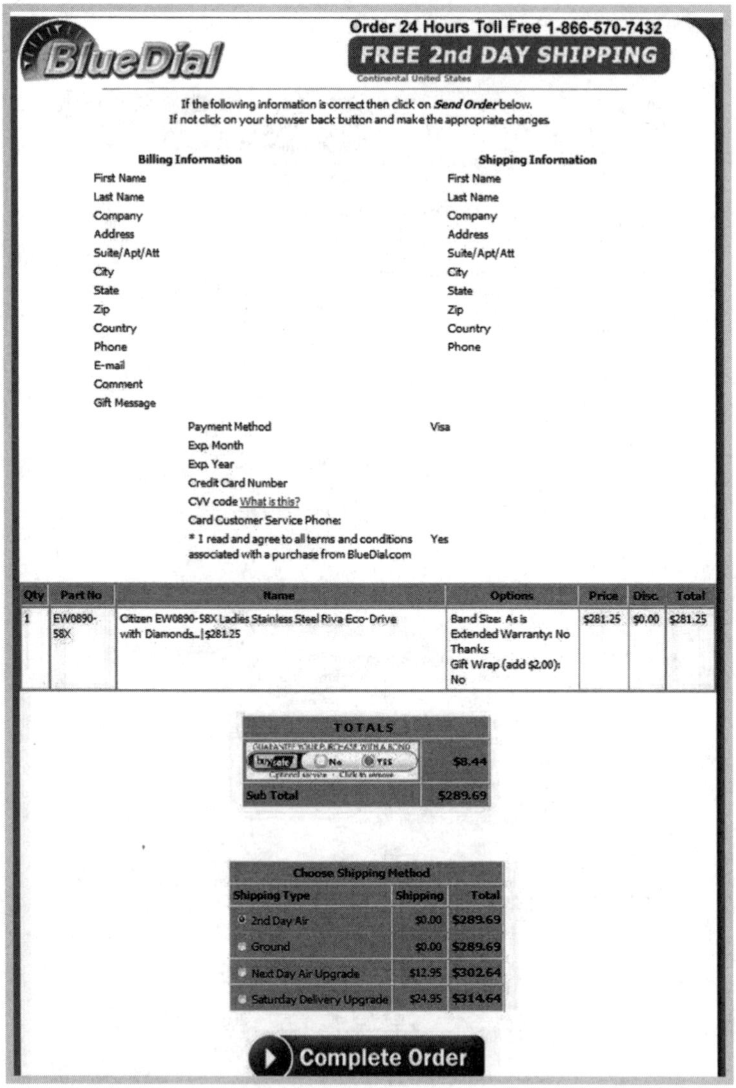

Figure 11.17. Shipping and billing confirmation

Step 5. Thank-You Page

The final page of the process (Figure 11.18) is the thank-you page with your order confirmation number and information indicating that your credit card transaction was processed successfully. Following this there is more information on how to contact the Web site, and notification that you qualify for a reward if you agree to review and rate the Web site. This is an excellent placement of survey information, as it does not interrupt the shopping experience, yet it still encourages you to leave feedback almost immediately. It also ensures that most of the feedback the Web site receives will be positive. By going through the checkout process successfully, users will generally be happy with the procedure, and putting a survey in front of happy users frequently garners positive reviews for sellers.

Figure 11.18. Thank-you page

In addition to the standard confirmation e-mail with product, shipping, and other information, this Web site also sends an e-mail explaining the bonding process (Figure 11.19). Given that many items on this site can be highly priced, you would most likely respond well to the extra assurance that your order is protected. If there is a problem when you receive the order, you can make a claim through this third party to get your money back. The information contained here also clearly tells you whom to contact and what the deadlines are. All in all, it's an excellent follow-up and postsale touch point.

Figure 11.19. Bonding process

Now that you've seen some examples of other Web site's shopping carts, let's take a look at some potential problems facing *your* site's checkout experience.

■ ■ ■ Shopping Cart Abandonment

Now that you've seen some examples of other Web sites' shopping carts, let's take a look at some potential problems facing *your* site's checkout experience.

Shopping cart abandonment is one of the leading areas in which online retailers invest when trying to increase revenues. Nothing is worse than seeing reports showing that your users put products into their shopping carts, started to process their checkout, then left the site completely. Yes, a small percentage might return to complete their intended purchase, but, for the most paut, once users bail out at this point in the process, they're gone for good.

Why People Abandon Shopping Carts

In this section we'll examine common reasons for shopping cart abandonment and things you can do to solve the problems.

Price-Related Concerns

One of the most common reasons shopping carts are abandoned is simply that the price was too high. While many manufacturers will require you to show the manufacturer's suggested retail price (MSRP) they have for a product, some Web sites will show lower prices. For your site, you should consider instituting a price match guarantee policy. This tells users you are willing to match a lower advertised price from an authorized dealer (protecting you from having to match prices with gray market Web sites) and eliminates a major fear users have: "What if I could get it cheaper elsewhere?" Many users state that the reason they left the shopping cart was because they simply wanted to do comparison shopping. They needed to go through the process to the end to understand what the final cost to them was going to be before checking out how much it would cost elsewhere.

Sometimes, users will be satisfied with the price of the product, only to discover that the shipping cost is too high. Establishing the shipping costs early on for users can help them better understand what to expect. If you feel you should operate the shipping cost line item as a profit center, think again. This isn't eBay, where the product is a penny and the shipping $15. Your shipping costs should be as low as they can be. If your competitors have minimal shipping charges and you do not, they will quickly take your business.

Errors on the Site

Sometimes Web sites make the mistake of not offering enough payment options. I'm still surprised when I encounter sites that accept only PayPal (or sites that *refuse* to accept PayPal, for that matter). Now, substitute Visa, MasterCard, and American Express for PayPal, and the result is just as crazy. Do not limit your shoppers to only certain payment methods. Many banks now allow direct payment from a user's bank account, so you should make this option available too. Targeting the major credit cards, direct-to-bank options, and PayPal will usually cover you for most transactions, but look to your users. If they generally prefer an alternate form of payment, for whatever reason, you'd better get it hooked up, and fast.

Another mistake that affects some Web sites is a glitch that brings up the wrong product. In many cases, it's an inventory issue, but it always has the effect of turning off shoppers. Users select items they want, but for whatever reason, while the models might be the same, they're not in the color the users want. Better to be clear, as in the ShopNBC examples seen in Figures 11.20 and 11.21, about what you do and do not have.

Figure 11.20. Display page—in stock

Also, nothing puts shoppers off as much as having to go through the entire shopping process only to discover that an item is back-ordered or sold out. The best place for this information is on the product page. If a product is back-ordered or sold out, the image and information should be changed to reflect this situation, ensuring that shoppers know what's up before they even try to start a checkout process. Figure 11.20 shows that the blue watch is in stock, and Figure 11.21 shows that the black watch is sold out. These figures are excellent examples of how to manage user expectations.

Figure 11.21. Display page—sold out

Technical difficulties with the system can also cause users to abandon their shopping carts. Make sure your shopping cart system works flawlessly . . . every time. If users encounter an error, they will think it's a waste of time to do anything further with your site and will leave to shop elsewhere. If you are aware of an error, fix it immediately. Also make sure to set up a warning or error alert system so that the system can flag errors when they occur.

Other Concerns

Sometimes users leave shopping carts behind because they are confused by the Web site. The problem could be unclear navigation, too many messages on a page, limited directions, or difficulty understanding options, but when potential buyers get confused, many choose to leave rather than try to figure it all out.

Other users may leave because of impatience. If they have a poor connection or are naturally impatient, there is nothing you can do with your Web site to entice these users further. However, slow load times and a lack of clarity on your end can easily frustrate users, *making* them impatient. When users feel frustrated while trying to give their money to a business, they usually leave.

Also, if users are unsure about whether your Web site is safe, secure, and trustworthy, they'll leave to shop elsewhere. While your Web site might have the latest logos plastered all over it from security firms that have vetted your trustworthiness, make sure your shopping cart process possesses the same "feel good" level about security. If, upon checkout, users get the feeling that you are anything less than 100 percent legitimate, they will abandon their shopping carts immediately.

In the next section, we will address all the above issues, and you'll learn some ways to ensure that users won't bail out.

■ ■ ■ Minimizing Shopping Cart Abandonment

This should be a major area of focus for you. If you've managed to move people this far in the sales funnel, it's a terrible waste to lose them and have to start over with a new sale or client. Pretty much everything that follows—simplicity, transparency, technology—is easy to accomplish with today's software and systems. By taking the time to explore each point as it relates to your own situation, you can create a checklist of action items.

Short of a mass infusion of traffic, fine-tuning your checkout process will probably be one of the single biggest things you can do to increase your conversion rates. If you're using a system you can customize, get started on that checklist. You'll need to be able to access the code that runs the system to manage any customization. If you use a third-party solution, this information will help you review your own process and provide a shopping list for an improved system to which you can migrate. If you have to pick a place to start your journey on improving conversion rates, the cart is an excellent spot. Let's take a run through the major points.

Simplicity

Think about how lean and streamlined your process can be: the bare minimum. Nothing extra, not an ounce of extra fat in the system anywhere. Now cut the entire thing in half. Can you do it? Seriously, you need to get tough with regard to simplifying your checkout process. You cannot make the system easy enough for users, so if there is any way to eliminate even one step, to remove even one piece of information, you should do it. The idea here is to ensure that users are not left to figure things out on their own. The next step should always be obvious to them and should require no special action or thought. As odd as it may seem, if you let users think, they'll get lost. Don't give them the chance.

Bread Crumb Navigation

Be sure to enable clear navigation in your shopping cart. "Bread crumb navigation" refers to those little clickable links that you see built near the tops of pages as you move through a Web site. The goal of these links is to provide an easy path for users to step back and forth between pages they have recently visited if they choose to. Your system should also remember users' information. There is nothing worse than filling in all the blanks, realizing you need to double-check something on the previous page, and when you return to the current page being faced with empty blanks again.

Don't Require Registration Before Shopping

By enabling a full shopping experience prior to registration, you not only increase your chances of making a sale, but also increase the chances of getting users to sign up. You can offer the option to "keep your information for registration" at the end of the checkout process on the thank-you page. Rest assured that users will be back if they liked shopping with you. If they miss the registration message this time, it'll be there for them the next time.

No Surveys During Checkout

Don't use the checkout process as a time to start a survey with users. It's distracting, and it may put them off. They are there to shop, so let them get on with it. If you feel the need to capture information about them, offer a link to a survey on the thank-you page with their confirmation information.

Setup and Testing

By the time you have your Web site up and running, and the checkout software humming along, you will be so familiar with the site that you're likely to miss small details. That's why it's crucial to run your own focus group by having others test the checkout process. Make sure you use people you know—family and friends, for example. Have them run through the entire process from front to back several times, selecting different products each time. The goal is to cover as much ground as possible with fresh eyes. Your testers will come back with reams of data for you regarding the little things you might have overlooked in the process. Make sure you take action on these things. This sort of testing is what separates an outstanding checkout process from a decent checkout process.

Transparency

Nothing helps close a sale like transparency. If your users can see every step of the process, can get all the information they need, know when there's a problem, and get in touch with you if need be, then they will be that much more likely to hand over their credit card information.

Be Accessible

Show your shoppers you care by allowing them access to you. If you want their money, a phone number to call to ask for help is a reasonable trade-off. At the very least there should be direct contact e-mails available to them. Today, though, there's no reason why businesses shouldn't explore options like remote call centers and live chat clients embedded in the process. The live chat clients are great ways to place customer support within one click for your users, as they function the way instant messenger services do, except, in this case, they give your users a chance to ask direct questions about your products and services and to receive answers immediately.

Shipping Information and Arrival Dates

Nothing secures a sale like telling shoppers they can have the product tomorrow. True, it takes a lot to make that happen, but the promise of quick shipping can increase sales dramatically. You need to be transparent about it, though. Amazon does a great job by showing a countdown in hours and minutes. If you place your order within that window, the item will arrive on the date shown if/when you select the appropriate shipping option. This is a powerful way to encourage sales and communicate clearly with users at the same time.

Polite Error Messages

Take the time to make sure your error messages are polite. If a user enters a four-digit zip code instead of a five-digit one, or if a user enters an obviously wrong phone number, ensure that your message about the error is friendly. People don't like to be told they made a mistake, and during the online checkout process, distractions and errors can be the kiss of death. The bottom line is to handle folks with kid gloves. Be gentle. Politely inform them that there seems to be an issue with the last information they entered and would they kindly please review it for accuracy.

Hidden or Extra Costs

Never hold back any information around the final cost of an item. Shipping, handling, currency conversion rates, gift-wrapping options, insurance, and any other charges should all be openly displayed and calculated for early in the process. The final review stage is not the place for users to suddenly learn of extra fees or costs.

Security

People love to feel protected during the shopping process, so make sure you clearly show any security badges from relevant services to which your business subscribes. If you are serious about protecting your users' information, make sure you let them know as much by placing the badges in prominent places on all your pages. If you are processing orders on a nonsecure page (http:// instead of https://), please stop. Today's Secure Socket Layer technologies help protect both your business and your users' information. Don't think about processing a transaction unless you are using a secure server.

Technology

Technology and software evolve at a rapid pace, and improvements in security and processing options are constant.

Shopping Cart Software

Ensure that you have the latest version of your shopping cart system software. Even a system just a few years old may have flaws that can be exploited, so staying current with your software helps protect both you and your users. In addition, newer editions often have more features to enable a richer user experience, which can help increase conversions.

Think Globally

Incorporate currency conversion tools plainly and obviously. The nature of the Internet means that those visiting your Web site will end up hailing from around the globe. While most will likely come from one main region, why make it difficult for the rest of the world's shoppers to transact business? Having a free currency converter on your site is simple to manage. Most shopping carts today can also handle the conversion information as part of the transaction, so enable that.

Warnings and Errors

Make sure your system is not showing errors. Users will often misread these warning messages (in most cases triggered by their browsers) to mean there is a safety concern with the Web site. Something as simple as calling an image from a non-secure site with Internet Explorer can cause such an error to appear. Don't leave things to chance. Make sure you fully test your system thoroughly in both Firefox and Internet Explorer.

Other Points to Consider

Here are some other things to consider about your Web site and the shopping experience.

Images and Information

Pictures sell products. No mystery there. Be sure, though, to keep the checkout process fast by using smaller images in this space. Slowing the process by using larger images that load more slowly can turn folks off in a big way and cause them to leave. If you feel the need to show a larger image and more detailed information, create a page that houses the information or reuse the Web site product page with the image already intact. Just be sure that when you reference this information, you place a link in the checkout process that opens a new window. You do not want users taken away from the current checkout process window.

Bells and Whistles

Upsells and cross-selling opportunities can reside inside the checkout process. These are valid, valuable ways to increase sales. What should not reside inside this process are things such as links to other sites, advertising banners, newsletter sign-up links, and the like. The list of what should be seen inside a checkout process is short—don't try to reinvent it. Upsell, yes. Cross-sell, yes. Other revenue-generating items, no.

How Much Is the Right Amount?

There is a lot to consider when operating your own online sales system. Users want to feel safe and secure; you must guide them and know how much information is the right amount to present to them. The process needs to be short and reliable. Make sure to set up a dedicated feedback loop specifically around your checkout process. This can include an exit survey on the confirmation page or even a survey that targets select users and rewards them for completion via the follow-up confirmation e-mail. You need to politely correct them and always be an unseen, steady hand leading them to the next step. While you cannot reach into their wallets, by optimizing your checkout process, you can encourage them to want to reach into their wallets for you.

In the next chapter we'll take a look at why analytics are so important. We will also examine select options for smaller Web sites and larger Web sites. Included in the discussion will be information on analytic systems designed specifically to dig deep on search marketing data. While many may roll their eyes at the concept of trolling for reports looking for patterns from the numbers, this is one area you cannot afford to overlook if you run a business online. Analytics are the lifeblood of all Web sites and the foundation for making sound decisions around optimizing for conversions.

12

Analytics: Running the Numbers

ANALYTICS. STATS. The numbers. Doesn't matter much how you refer to this information, it just matters that you pay attention to it. By focusing carefully on what your analytics are telling you, a picture of how users are interacting with your Web site will emerge. This information, while it can be daunting and very detailed, is worth getting a handle on, as it is one of the clearest ways to help you make sound business decisions.

What's Important to You?

There is an overabundance of data to be derived from analytics, and an excellent way to cut down on the clutter is to determine up front which key performance indicators (KPIs) matter most to you. By focusing on only these few elements of information, you can begin to quickly and easily track trends and gain insight into user behavior. Typically, Web sites look for information about the following points:

- Unique visitors
- Page views

- Time spent on site
- Entry and exit points
- Conversions (of course)
- ROI (return on investment)

The degree to which you value each of these is completely your choice. Given that my own Web sites are advertising based for revenue generation, I value unique visitors, time on site, and page views. From this I can gain an understanding of how users are interacting with my Web site and also judge the effectiveness of my search marketing efforts to capture new traffic. Everything else I need to know is provided via Google AdSense in the form of revenue reporting. In fact, I have my own analytics review process distilled to where I reference only Google AdSense to determine visits, page views, and revenue generated on a daily, weekly, and monthly basis. I do maintain a full suite of analytics for those times when I need to dig deeper to uncover opportunities or investigate failures, but through trial and error I have found which analytics (which KPIs) are most meaningful to me.

■ ■ ■ Options

There are analytics suites available for every demand, from the smallest Web sites to the largest publishers. In fact, with today's technologies you would have to work hard to not find analytics of some sort for your situation. While it is not possible to offer reviews on every analytics suite available today, let's take a basic look at which options are available.

Smaller and Medium Web Sites

For smaller Web sites, you can easily get information by accessing Google Analytics. This is an excellent system, which, when activated on your Web site, will begin giving you daily updates of critical data points. The information is easy to understand, well categorized, and exportable. By placing a small piece of JavaScript code on your Web site, Google can gather an almost endless amount of information about your traffic statistics. You should not fear Google's gathering this information, as it is collected solely for the purpose of sharing with you through their analytics system. It remains contained within your own account login, and safe from public view.

One advantage to Google Analytics is the ease with which you can integrate Google AdWords into the system to get a true view of what your ROI looks like. This return on investment information is calculated by the system tracking your ad spending on AdWords and the conversion information captured by Google Analytics. The result is end-to-end tracking of your spending and whether it is converting or not. This is one of the reasons why Google Analytics is such a popular choice with many small and medium-sized Web sites.

■ ■ ■ ONLINE RESOURCE ■ ■ ■

Two more options for smaller and medium-sized Web sites would be AWStats (awstats.sourceforge.net) and OneStat.com. There are plenty of other options available to you, and, in many cases, if you are hosting a Web site, you should check with your Web hosting company to see what options are available through it. Today most reputable hosts will provide statistics of some sort when you rent a server or space on a server from them.

Larger Publishers

For the larger publishers who need systems capable of handling millions of page views per day, probably the best choices are Omniture (www.omniture.com) and Webtrends (www.webtrends.com). Either system is capable of handling Web sites of this scale and running reports reliably. Both systems also cost quite a bit of money for monthly access and will require a detailed understanding of their unique setup needs. While both are incredibly powerful in preparing reports, there is a learning curve to understanding how best to gather information within these systems. If you are in the market for systems such as these, you should ask how to integrate revenue information into the systems so that you can see your ROI from one reporting interface.

Search Marketing Platforms

In today's world, where search marketing plays such an important role in traffic generation and conversions, there are platforms available to contract specifically search-related information. Two standouts in this category are Conductor (www.conductor.com) and Enquisite (www.enquisite.com). While bulls take a slightly different approach to tracking search marketing, both offer insights that common analytics fail to reach. The level of detail these systems can track and categorize in search marketing campaigns is truly impressive. These systems allow you to get down to a keyword level and understand if variations between plurals and singulars drive conversions. Reporting offered from both systems is also designed in a manner that produces more readily understood outputs. Being able to see results clearly in side-by-side graphs makes it easier for you to understand where your performing keywords lie.

Log Files

You should also take the time to look through your own server log files in your search for Web site analytics. While this information will not appear in a visually pleasing manner, it is worth looking through because it will provide you with a wealth of information about your Web site and your users. Your server tracks every single action it executes and every request made of it. By looking through these "logs," you can find useful information and see trends based on how users interact with your Web site. It is also 100 percent free, since this information is captured by your server anyway. Your log files will not provide information on conversions, however, unless you know exactly which pages indicate that a conversion has taken place. For example, if each conversion on your Web site shows users a thank-you page at the end of their purchase, your server log files will note how many times that individual page was shown on a given date. You could then see that a conversion occurred by looking in your server log files. This will not show you data on revenue, however.

■ ■ ■ Some Words of Caution

No matter which system you use, take care to craft individual campaigns to track the effectiveness of all of the variety of conversion options across your Web site. By setting up individual campaigns and using individual tracking tags (little pieces of code that help your analytics system identify an individual page) on your pages, you can understand which versions of body copy or page variants are generating sales. Look for analytics packages, which help you do A/B and split testing (tracking multiple options). This ability helps you see which options are performing well and which ones you should turn off.

You should also take care to ensure that the tracking tags you install in the code of your pages are placed on the correct pages. This is often the thank-you page users see, which summarizes the purchases they have just completed. Often these tracking tags are placed in the wrong location, artificially inflating conversion numbers, which subsequently do not match up with revenue numbers.

While there are no hard and fast rules that explain how much traffic a Web site should generate, in the world of search marketing, there are some basic expectations. Organic search marketing generally starts to yield results after a few months, and if you continue your organic search optimization, you can expect to see traffic increase further after about one year. Paid search campaigns will yield traffic almost immediately, but as discussed earlier in the book, you have to carefully weigh the value of this traffic against your conversions to ensure that you are running at a net positive ROI. Overall, you should be looking for an increase each month in your inbound referrals from all sources. The goal, obviously, is a graph that trends upward. Never assume the amount of traffic you are receiving is what you should be receiving. Always look for ways to increase traffic and increase conversions. Your analytics will help you understand what the bigger picture around users interacting with your Web site looks like.

You can easily spend half of each day trying to improve your Web site by studying your analytics. As you establish your KPIs, you'll develop a muscle memory for finding information quickly. After some exposure to this information, you'll begin to see and understand the trends of your Web site and your users, and any variations will stand out. I cannot stress enough how important it is to have your analytics set up correctly and operating properly before you start making decisions on how to change things on your Web site in your quest to increase conversions.

You need to make sure you're seeing data in your system. Be certain your analytics code is correctly installed in the code of your Web site's pages and take the time to set up the analytics system itself to show you data you want to see. Many systems allow you to customize what data is shown to you, so taking the time to do this will help manage the flow of the data you need in order to make decisions. When your analytics are running at 100 percent, showing you the KPI data you want to see, tracking your pages properly, and giving you ROI data, you will be in a position to start making decisions from solid information. While not glamorous, analytics are the heart of business.

In the next chapter you will find a series of interviews with Web pioneers and online conversion experts. There is an excellent cross section of Web entrepreneurs and service providers. All have long and successful careers in making money online, either directly through their own Web sites or by operating businesses that help Web sites optimize their conversion processes. So turn the page and let's see what the successful Web entrepreneurs have to say about turning clicks into conversions.

13

Industry Expert Interviews: Direct Advice and Insights from Successful People

I REACHED OUT TO some of the big names in search, online marketing, and conversion optimization, and in this chapter we will discuss what matters with regard to increasing conversions. Each of the experts interviewed was asked the same questions, and, as you'll see, they all have slightly different takes on things. One common thread is testing. It doesn't matter what else you might be doing, if you are not testing your site and working to improve from the results, you're not doing everything you can to truly optimize for conversions.

In order of appearance, the list of interviewees is:

- Jeremy Schoemaker: founder of ShoeMoney Capital and shoppingads.com
- Khalid Saleh: founder of Invesp.com, a conversion rate optimization company

- Ben Jesson and Karl Blanks: cofounders of Conversion Rate Experts, a leading UK conversion optimization company
- Rand Fishkin: founder of the successful search optimization company SEOMoz.com
- Rae Hoffman: successful Internet entrepreneur who runs Outspoken Media and bbgeeks.com
- Stephan Spencer: founder of Netconcepts, a leading search optimization company

These folks run some of the most successful search optimization, online marketing, and conversion optimization businesses today. Some also have stand-alone Web sites that are leaders in their verticals and that have been successfully monetized. This chapter will offer you a broader view of conversion optimization and leave you with solid leads about where to turn next. Some of you will want to follow along on the blogs these people maintain. Others of you may need more in-depth assistance. Now you know where to start looking.

■ ■ ■ Jeremy Schoemaker

Founder of www.auctionads.com (now shoppingads.com) and ShoeMoney Capital, a company that funds small start-ups.

Tell us a little about yourself, your business, and how you came to be doing what you do now.

In the early 2000s I started a Web site where people could submit their own cell phone wallpapers and ring tones and share them with the world. It gained enormous popularity very fast, and before long I got a call from a rep at Google who told me about a new product it had called AdSense. I tried its monetization products, and, within a couple months, I was making over $100,000 a month from Google AdSense alone. I was pretty fascinated with how monetizing Web sites worked, so I started playing around with other forms of revenue, such as subscriptions, donations, and even doing my own product sales.

While doing this, I started my own blog where I chronicled my adventures in trying to learn how to make money on the Internet, at www.shoemoney.com. The blog gained in readership, and eventually I leveraged that into starting my own display advertising company called AuctionAds.

AuctionAds was built around the eBay affiliate system. Seeing that eBay has inventory for virtually every possible niche there is, and since it is located in over 12 countries, with AuctionAds my company created the most diversified advertising platform ever seen. Less than four months after we launched the advertising network we had over 25,000 active users doing millions per month in revenue, and then we sold the company.

After selling AuctionAds, I leveraged the capital from the sale to invest in several Internet start-ups and form what is now known as ShoeMoney Capital.

I still continue to write the blog at shoemoney.com, do a lot of affiliate marketing, and look for opportunities to invest in new Internet start-ups.

We all understand the importance of optimizing a Web site to generate traffic, but how about optimizing a site for conversions? Why does this critical step seem to be an overlooked practice by most Web site owners?

If you're not optimizing a Web site to convert your goals, then you're wasting your time and resources. Optimizing a Web site for search is fine once you have your goals dialed in. I can't tell you how many people I know who start this process in reverse, optimizing their Web site for search keywords and then later trying to optimize for conversions. To me it does not matter what my keywords rank for if they are not helping me accomplish my goals.

What are the most common obstacles to conversion success you see on Web sites today?

By far the most common obstacle to conversion success is simply that people don't understand what their goal is. For instance when you ask most people what their goal is, they will just tell you "to make money." You really have to drill down your goals much more granular than that. For example, if you own a *shoe* Web site, your first goal is to get users to the product page, then to the checkout page, and then actually have them complete that process. Now, there are many points of failure along each of these goal paths. You should try to optimize for every step in order to get to the next phase of your goal.

When you approached your last project, what did your plan for optimizing for conversions look like? What critical items had to be covered in the project?

One of our newest products is called ShoeMoney Tools. This is an Internet marketing suite of search engine optimization [SEO], Pay Per Click [PPC], and other tools to help Internet marketers make more money. One of our biggest challenges in conversion for this Web site was that a lot of our biggest competitors were fly-by-night scammy Web sites promising riches for no work. To anyone who was not familiar with our brand, it was very hard to convince users they should sign up for our tools at $99 per month when this other product was out there for free with $4.95 shipping and handling. Now, the other product is going to charge users for the rest of their lives at crazy rates, but they don't know this at the start. The client gets lured in by the low up-front cost promise.

Our challenge was to familiarize people with our brand, so we created a free 12-week training course at shoemoneyx.com that goes through every in and out of Internet marketing. Throughout this free course we demonstrate how to use our tools and others' tools and how they help you. This brings trust with our brand and greatly increased our sign-ups.

Based on your own experiences, which of the main channels have worked best in terms of generating traffic that converts?

I would say that in every case paid search always works the best to start. It's the easiest way to understand which specific keywords are going to give you the best return on investment. Also because you can increase volume very easily, you can test lots of variations in landing pages for conversion. You can then take this data and optimize your SEO and social media campaigns.

Please share with us three things readers can apply to their own Web sites today to help them increase conversions.

The first must-have product is Google Website Optimizer, which will rotate various images, landing page copy, and several other things to help you hone in on the perfect landing page for your products.

Kissmetrics.com/CrazyEgg.com is an excellent product that shows you a heat map of where your users are clicking. When you have your landing page style, then this data is crucial if you're going to do any changes.

Google Analytics: all marketers have everything they need in their numbers with this system. You can read about other people's techniques all you want, but what's going to work best for you is in your own analytics. I like to use Google Analytics, but there are tons of other awesome products for free.

Any other words of wisdom to share with readers with regard to increasing conversions?

One of the biggest keys in optimizing for conversion is just doing a ton of testing on all levels. Never give up on testing, never stop testing. It takes time, but it's a wise investment of time.

■ ■ ■ Khalid Saleh

Founder of Invesp.com, a company specializing in conversion rate optimization for online businesses.

Tell us a little about yourself, your business, and how you came to be doing what you do now.

My name is Khalid Saleh. I am the cofounder and president of Invesp, a conversion rate optimization company. We focus on e-commerce conversion rate optimization by helping e-commerce companies convert their Web site traffic into actual orders. I have been working with e-commerce companies since 1995. Over the last 15 years I noticed that most e-commerce Web sites focused on bringing visitors to their sites and paid little attention to how these visitors react to the site. The culminating point was when I led a project for one of my clients with a $15 million budget, building the latest and greatest e-commerce platform. The site had tens of thousands of visitors the first day it went live but fewer than 10 orders. I knew at that point that conversion optimization is where I should focus my energy.

We all understand the importance of optimizing a Web site to generate traffic, but how about optimizing a site for conversions? Why does this critical step seem to be an overlooked practice by most Web site owners?

I wrote an article about this previously: www.seo-scoop.com/2007/08/27/why-do-we-accept-low-conversion-rates/. I will summarize the main points:

- Conversion data can be difficult to track: for pure e-commerce operations, it is easy to track orders. However, companies running a mixed operation (online and offline) report that offline sales increase as a result of their online presence. In that case, consumers complete the research online but the actual purchase (conversion) takes place in the physical store. So although the reported online conversion rate is low, the overall conversion rate for the company is actually higher.
- Traffic used to be cheap: the cost per visitor was minimal 10 years ago. That is not the case anymore, but many companies are stuck in their ways.
- Increasing conversion is tricky: increasing online conversion is part science, part art. It is the intersection of the creative, marketing, and analytical disciplines. Picking the wrong area to start with can produce negative impact. Not done correctly, Web site operators can reduce their conversion rates even further.

What are the most common obstacles to conversion success you see on Web sites today?

Perhaps the biggest blocker to conversion is trust and confidence. If you operate a Web site with a well-known brand name, then this is not an issue you have to contend with. But that is not the case for 99.99 percent of the Web sites out there. People will not place an order with you or hand you their private information until they feel they can trust you, your products, and your services. Trust, of course, is a very general term, and it translates into over 70 or so factors that impact how visitors react to a Web site.

Another common error is not defining the conversion goal clearly. A typical Web site will have multiple conversion goals, but there should be one primary goal and objective. Defining that goal and building different pages so that all elements support the primary goal will persuade the user to convert.

Too many competing images and messages is another common error. People tend to get creative with their Web sites and think that more is better. Understanding how a user visualizes a Web page (eye-tracking) will help you realize that placing so many different images, text sizes, information, links, etc., will only confuse a user.

If you drive traffic to your Web site through PPC, then there are few other reasons why people do not convert on your site:

- Using a Web site's main home page as a landing page is a terrible mistake. You will be amazed how many Fortune 1000 companies spend millions of dollars on PPC ads, and when you click on these ads, you're navigated to the main home page of the site. They are expecting users to look around the site and find what they are looking for. That does not happen.
- Lack of continuity between the ad and the landing page itself. For example, the ad title may describe something that hooks users, but as soon as they click on the ad, they are navigated to a page that has no mention or relation to what the ad listed.

When you approached your last project, what did your plan for optimizing for conversions look like? What critical items had to be covered in the project?

Since we work strictly with conversion optimization, here is the general approach we take:

- Analytics analysis: look at the numbers behind the site and determine which areas are the best candidates for optimization.
- Persona development: take the different marketing data and translate that into different personas that represent the different segments you are targeting via the Web site.

- Utilize the analytics and persona information to start optimizing different pages on the site in a systematic process.
- Make small changes and test their effectiveness and the impact they have on conversion rate.

Based on your own experiences, which of the main channels have worked best in terms of generating traffic that converts?

I would have to say that paid search done correctly produces the best traffic that converts. This is followed closely by well-optimized organic traffic. Social media traffic is the hardest to convert in the typical sense of conversion.

Please share with us three things readers can apply to their own Web sites today to help them increase conversions.

- Headlines and copy: Your messages have to be razor sharp in that they consider users from every perspective, buying stage, and persona type. Headlines and copy throughout need to solve the users' problems and persuade them to select your service/product over the rest of the competition.
- An image is worth a thousand words, including the fact that an image is important because it can support the message you are trying to send to users. However, keep it real and direct, and don't get fancy with Adobe's Flash. Simplicity is more often the solution to a better optimized page.
- Don't ask too much of your site visitors: too many lead generation Web sites ask their visitors to fill out the forms with information that could be captured later, when a sales person actually talks to the lead. Filling contact forms should be as quick and easy as possible for the visitor. The less time users must spend on your conversion activity, the less time they have to change their minds. And never put a "Clear Form" button next to the "Submit" button.
- Don't get carried away: Resist the temptation to use the latest Web graphic effects merely because they are the latest. Simple is better. The

focus of your page needs to be completely on getting visitors to perform the desired action. Using too much technology will distract them, and your message may be lost.

Any other words of wisdom to share with the readers with regard to increasing conversions?

Conversion optimization is a continuous process of improvement. It is not something that should be done once and you are finished. I have seen clients go from a 4 percent conversion rate to a conversion rate greater than 14 percent through careful analysis, careful implementation, and continuous optimization. Some Web site owners think it is impossible to achieve such results. That is simply not true. Other Web site owners get carried away trying to test thousands of combinations and end up frustrated along the way. Plan your optimization effort and execute carefully, and you should see improvement.

■ ■ ■ Ben Jesson and Karl Blanks

Ben and Karl are the cofounders of Conversion Rate Experts, a leading UK conversion optimization company whose client list includes Sony, Vodafone, 888.com, British Telecom, and more.

Tell us a little about yourselves, your business, and how you came to be doing what you do now.

In December 2006 Karl (a former rocket scientist!) and I launched a Web site called www.conversion-rate-experts.com, which contained a single-page report called "Google Website Optimizer 101."

The article revealed some of the techniques we'd developed when we tripled the size of an online international telecom company. The report went viral thanks to social bookmarking Web sites like Digg.com and Delicious.com, and was featured on the Alexa "Movers and Shakers" list as the third fastest-growing Web site in the world.

The following day we were contacted by Google, which suggested we partner with it to offer consulting services. Google invited us to become the first European consulting partner for its Web site optimizer service.

Since then we have had some fantastic successes for clients in some highly competitive industries, including business to business, e-commerce, weight loss, travel, gaming, technology, and health and fitness. Our client portfolio now includes Sony, Vodafone, British Telecom, 888.com, SEOmoz, and SEO Book.

We all understand the importance of optimizing a Web site to generate traffic, but how about optimizing a site for conversions? Why does this critical step seem to be an overlooked practice by most Web site owners?

I think many marketers believe that the easiest way to increase sales is to just get more traffic. But to invest in traffic (whether using PPC or investing in SEO), you need to be able to outbid everyone else who wants that traffic. And you can only afford to outbid them if you are able to outmonetize them. In other words, *you need to be able to extract more profit from that traffic than anyone else can.*

That's what we do: we redesign companies' sales funnels so they become incredibly effective at turning traffic into money—at converting visitors into spenders.

The obvious upside to this is that your sales increase. But the less obvious—and more powerful—upside is that you become able to spend more on traffic than all your competitors (on channels like SEO, PPC, affiliate programs, and offline marketing). Many successful companies—such as Amazon, eBay, and Expedia—have brilliantly effective sales funnels, so buying traffic becomes easy for them. But only because they put enormous effort into optimizing their user experience, so they are great at turning visitors into spenders.

What are the most common obstacles to conversion success you see on Web sites today?

Here's the big problem with conversion rate optimization: if you want to make your Web site better at turning visitors into customers (or leads/subscribers/members), you need to understand why most of your visitors are leaving! But those people come and go without trace! How do you know what they wanted? How do you know what would have persuaded them to take action?

If you owned a real-life bricks-and-mortar store, this would be easy: You'd hear their objections. You'd be able to ask questions. You'd hear what they muttered as they headed for the door.

Capturing the voice-of-the-customer is more difficult online (which is perhaps why so many people focus on driving more traffic), but it *can* be done if you use the right tools and techniques.

For example, exit surveys help you understand why people came to your Web site and why they left. Tools such as Live Chat allow you to gather questions and objections from your visitors. You can then test incorporating the answers and counter-objections into your content (we call with process O/CO = objection/counterobjection).

When you approached your last project, what did your plan for optimizing for conversions look like? What critical items had to be covered in the project?

We follow a process we've developed called Conversion Rate Optimization. Here's a sneak preview of our approach:

- Understanding (and tuning) our client's long-term strategy for dominating the market: this is vital when starting a conversion project, so you work on the right areas of the business—and not just short-term goals/fixes.
- Understanding and experimenting with existing traffic sources: it's important to consider the different types of visitors to a Web site, where they came from, what they are looking for, and whether they have visited your Web site before. All these things affect what the optimal conversion funnel should look like.
- Understanding your visitors (in particular the nonconverting ones): if you don't know why your visitors don't take action, you can fix it!
- Competitive research and market intelligence: Where does your product/service/company fit into the marketplace. Does this position fit with your core strengths and long-term strategy?

- Prioritizing your ideas: you need to know which test plans will have the biggest impact on conversion for the minimum effort.
- Designing your experimental Web pages (or page elements): this is the content that you will test against your existing Web site. Making these pages more persuasive, believable, and user friendly is vital for success.
- Carrying out experiments on your Web site: we use tools such as Google Website Optimizer to split test pages or page elements and measure which performs best.
- Finally, transferring your winning campaigns into other media: your increased conversion rate will mean you can profitably advertise in different media—such as PPC, affiliate marketing, or offline—which means your business will be much more stable. And because the content has been voted for by real prospects, you already know it's going to be more effective than adverts that haven't been tested.

Based on your own experiences, which of the main channels have worked best in terms of generating traffic that converts?

Referral traffic (from tell-a-friend programs, for example) and affiliate traffic where the prospect is presold on the product convert extremely well. One thing to consider is how to treat different types of visitors depending on their intent and stage of the buying process.

Please share with us three things readers can apply to their own Web sites today to help them increase conversions.

Find out why your prospects aren't taking action, fix those problems, and use split testing (that is, show the old version of the page to half of your visitors and the new version to the other half, and see which version gets the most orders).

Any other words of wisdom to share with the readers with regard to increasing conversions?

Speak with your sales people—or customer support people. They understand your customers in much more depth than any Web analytics report could. They know what the customers care about and what their major objections are. If you have no customer support people, consider temporarily adding a phone number to your Web site just to give yourself an opportunity to speak with customers.

■ ■ ■ Rand Fishkin

Rand is one of the founders of SEOmoz, a world-class search optimization firm based in Seattle. Rand's expertise extends beyond search marketing, however, and the SEOmoz client list includes companies such as Microsoft, National Public Radio, Fast Company, and more.

Tell us a little about yourself, your business, and how you came to be doing what you do now.

I'm 30 years old, married to an amazing woman, live in Seattle, and currently serve as the CEO of SEOmoz. The company is a fairly classic technology start-up: we've got 21 employees, a small amount of venture capital investment, and high hopes that we can take a process [the SEO process] that has been historically centered around consulting and fill some of those needs with software.

I started in the Web world in high school, building Web sites and playing around on bulletin boards and forums. From 1997 to 2002, my mom, Gillian, and I worked together to build sites and do small Web usability and interaction design contracts for local companies around the Puget Sound. In 2003, as our clients' needs centered more and more around SEO, we learned that practice and employed it with little success. The SEOmoz.org Web site was actually a side project launched in 2004 to help explain the challenges and opportunities I'd found through SEO. If you go back and read the blog from those days, you'll see a pretty ignorant kid writing about his trials and tribulations with the practice.

After a few years of blogging, the site became quite popular. We'd had some tools custom built for us to help accomplish basic SEO tasks, and I put those on the site with free access. As the community grew to thousands of daily visits, we knew that the consulting business we'd built around SEOmoz wasn't the way to scale long term. Thus, we created "PRO Membership"—the self-service SaaS [Software as a Service] product that drives 80-plus percent of revenue today.

In 2007 we started on the insanely challenging task of building our own representative index of the World Wide Web to help gain visibility and insight into the same kinds of metrics the search engines can see. We launched that project—Linkscape—in October 2008 and have been growing dramatically ever since. Paid membership to the site doubled from 2007 to 2008 and has already more than tripled now. Today we're serving 400K-plus visits each month and millions of requests to Linkscape's application programming interface (commonly known as API) for metrics like mozRank and link counts via a number of services. It's been a wild ride, but I suspect the toughest challenges are still to come.

We all understand the importance of optimizing a Web site to generate traffic, but how about optimizing a site for conversions? Why does this critical step seem to be an overlooked practice by most Web site owners?

To be honest, I really don't have a good answer here. At SEOmoz, we ignored this crucial piece plenty ourselves, not understanding that getting traffic to the site was only half the battle. For the last nine months we've employed the crew from Conversion Rate Experts [CRE] to help improve, and it's done dramatic things for the business. We've become much more focused on this piece of the puzzle, and now have processes in place to help design, launch, and iterate to achieve greater results.

What are the most common obstacles to conversion success you see on Web sites today?

Clear communication of a single message has to be at the top of the list. So many Web sites (and home pages in particular) try to fit so much in that the actual purpose of the site/page is entirely lost. We're not all Yahoo!, but so many of us still design from the "portal" perspective. A page doesn't need to be all things to all people; that's what search and navigation are for. A page's purpose should be distinct, obvious, and easily understood by any visitor.

When you approached your last project, what did your plan for optimizing for conversions look like? What critical items had to be covered in the project?

We've begun to focus on a few specific items: the purpose of the page, the call to action, and the supporting information. We build initial versions of each of these, iterate with our team and the CRE consultants, launch, test, and refine. It's not an easy process by any means, but then, if it was easy, I suppose everyone would be doing it well :-).

Based on your own experiences, which of the main channels have worked best in terms of generating traffic that converts?

Our own opt-in e-mail list has the highest conversion rates, followed by organic search, then social media. We don't currently use any paid search or banner advertising, though I know from our clients' projects that PPC is a good channel for conversion rate, though it can be exorbitantly expensive.

Please share with us three things readers can apply to their own Web sites today to help them increase conversions.

Show your wire-framed landing page ideas to a few current customer prospects and ask for their feedback. Listen carefully, don't defend your ideas, and be welcoming to criticism—you want to hear their objections.

Make two piles: things you like and/or want on your Web site and/or pages, and things you can improve, using data that will actually convert your visitors into customers. Note how distinct they are. Now use this evidence to refute any and all "But, the boss wants . . . " excuses for the future. Data-driven organizations are the ones that have conversion rate optimization success.

Use the right tools.

Any other words of wisdom to share with readers with regard to increasing conversions?

Two quick things: Number one; don't forget that conversion rate optimization requires a ton of time and energy. You need to have someone on the UI engineering side of things ready to devote lots of their daily effort to it, or else the process will take forever to get implemented. Number two, your brand is still important. Be careful that you're not sacrificing who you are and what you want to be for higher conversions; yes, data may tell you that superaggressive copy has a higher conversion rate initially, but you need to watch cohort analysis and temporal patterns to be sure you're not sacrificing long-term success for short-term gains.

■ ■ ■ Rae Hoffman

Rae Hoffman is an Internet entrepreneur. She has run a number of stand-alone Web sites and now runs MFE Interactive, which manages all her Web sites and OutSpoken Media. Both efforts keep her busy speaking at conferences year-round. If you own a BlackBerry, you might already know her BBGeeks.com Web site.

Tell us a little about yourself, your business, and how you came to be doing what you do now.

I fell into this industry completely by accident. After a long personal ordeal, I ended up founding the first international support group for parents and families of pediatric stroke survivors. I began my career in online marketing by trying to simply get the word out about the group to other parents.

By 2001, I was spending a lot of time running the group and started to wonder if there was a way to make money online. I fell into affiliate marketing, started to learn SEO, grasped the concept very quickly, and the rest, I guess, is history, or my history anyway. I've been making my full-time income online since 2002 via affiliate marketing, and I am best known online by my handle, Sugarrae.

In 2007, I left the land of "one man bands" and started a Web site publishing company called MFE Interactive, which is based in Guelph, Canada. MFE does what I did alone for many years, which is build affiliate sites, but we have a full-time staff of five, as well as several contractors that build, market, and monetize the sites under my direction. In 2009, I finally gave in to the demand I was experiencing for my consulting services by forming Outspoken Media with my partners Lisa Barone and Rhea Drysdale. I act as the CEO for both companies and also speak at various conferences all over the world trying to help others learn how to market their sites. It keeps me extremely busy as well as constantly challenged, and I wouldn't have it any other way.

We all understand the importance of optimizing a Web site to generate traffic, but how about optimizing a site for conversions? Why does this critical step seem to be an overlooked practice by most Web site owners?

I think a lot of people think if you can get the people to your site, everything else will fall into place. It's a common misconception. However, after you achieve rankings success, you quickly learn you need to focus on conversions to get every drop you can out of your online marketing budget. MFE Interactive owns a Web site called BBGeeks.com, and, in terms of traffic, it is one of the top sites on the Internet as far as a destination for BlackBerry owners.

But we quickly found that the site didn't convert as well as our other sites. So while it was the king of our brood as far as traffic, it was the redheaded stepchild when it came to earnings per visitor. Once we started seeing seven figures in page views each month, we quickly realized the biggest bang for our buck would be focusing on bettering the site conversions instead of being too heavily focused on gaining more traffic. Just because you build it and they come does not necessarily mean they'll buy. As an affiliate, I have spent many years focusing on converting the traffic I bring in, because affiliates only get paid via commissions on sales they generate. Our sites have to convert or we don't eat.

What are the most common obstacles to conversion success you see on Web sites today?

I think the biggest thing that makes me groan is when all the space "above the fold" is wasted on a graphic or Adobe Flash display. You have very little time to convince your site visitors you have what they're looking for. And unless you sell Web design or a single product, a graphic is likely not going to do it. The more times you make users click to get to what they want, the more you risk them getting bored, clicking the "Back" button, and moving on to the next site.

Other common issues we see are sites that require plug-ins to view and sites that fail to tell the user "what's in it for me." Your site visitors don't want to hear how fantastic you are. They want you to tell them how fantastic using your product or service (or one you recommend) will make their own lives. Some people call this concept features versus benefits. Features are important, but people typically buy based on benefits.

When you approached your last project, what did your plan for optimizing for conversions look like? What critical items had to be covered in the project?

Well, we've got a lot of experience at this point, and we have learned along the way what types of sites typically tend to convert best in which areas. For example, we'll never again "lead" a commercial/sales focused site with a blog (by that, I mean making the blog the home page). We use blogs to prop up the main site from a search engine optimization and word-of-mouth and viral marketing standpoint, but they are horrible, in our experience, when it comes to conversions focused around commercial products.

We also do a lot of click tracking. We want to know the exact link clicked that generated every single sale. It helps us identify patterns and see which links "work" and which links "don't." We use Crazyegg.com and find the data presented invaluable.

For instance, we have a site focused around fund-raising, and we found that of the three products we listed in the right sidebar, the third product was the one most clicked. Even though users had to look over the first two before reaching the third, the third consistently had the highest click-through rate. As a result, we moved the third product into the first position to make it easier to see (and click on), and we started testing new products in the second and third positions until we found ones that got higher click-through rates.

We had another site, and we were able to tell with click tracking that it was getting a lot of attempted clicks on graphics that were not "clickable." We made those graphics clickable to the proper pages and saw an increase in our earnings per visitor because people were able to more easily get to where they wanted to go, and more visitors started converting rather than getting confused by our "unclickable" graphics. Anything you can do to decrease user confusion or frustration will almost always increase your conversions.

In short, a lot of our focus is on tracking user behavior and making small changes, one at a time, and seeing what makes conversions go up (and keeping those implemented), and what makes them go down (and, as a result, removing whatever change we made).

Based on your own experiences, which of the main channels have worked best in terms of generating traffic that converts?

Well, first things first. I don't do any paid search. I've always been an organic girl. That said, when it comes to the various other online marketing methods—organic, video marketing, local search marketing, banner ads, social media, and the like, nothing converts for us like organic search does, especially "long tail" search terms.

That said, we've done quite a bit of testing in regards to conversions via social media, and we have found, based on the hard data, that Twitter is the highest converting social media outlet for our verticals, which are pretty spread out. Twitter consistently has a higher click-through rate on both "buy links" and "contextual advertising" on our sites. As a result, we put Twitter at the top of our social media marketing priorities for sites that are a fit for social media.

Please share with us three things readers can apply to their own Web sites today to help them increase conversions.

The first thing I'd recommend is implementing click tracking. As I mentioned above, we find the data incredibly valuable, and it will help you see your site through the eyes of a user. One problem a lot of site owners (or employees working on a site) experience is a sort of blindness to potential conversion pitfalls. You know where everything is and the site makes sense to you because you work with it every day. Your users are not as familiar with it, so anything you can do to get a glimpse of how they see the site will give you a ton of information to start testing with.

I'd also recommend some A/B testing, especially with site copy, so you can make changes and can make a valid interpretation of those changes. Your site on a Saturday is different than your site on a Monday, and your site in December might be different than your site in May. A/B testing allows you to split test, as accurately as possible, the effects of changes you make to your site.

Lastly, I'd recommend reading *Don't Make Me Think* by Steve Krug. It's a short read, but the information within it truly helps you understand regular Web users.

Any other words of wisdom to share with readers with regard to increasing conversions?

That's about all I've got for you. Test, test, test.

■ ■ ■ Stephan Spencer

Stephan Spencer is an old hand at online marketing and tuning for conversions. He founded Netconcepts and today enjoys a position in the industry as a thought leader and successful entrepreneur.

Tell us a little about yourself, your business, and how you came to be doing what you do now.

I founded Netconcepts in 1995 after dropping out of a Ph.D. program in biochemistry at the University of Wisconsin–Madison. I got my start on the Web by developing a Web site, just for fun, for my department at the university. Originally a Web design and development firm, Netconcepts evolved over the years into one of the leading search engine optimization firms, serving some of the largest brands in online retail. We span three continents—with offices in Madison, Auckland, and Beijing. In 2003, I invented Netconcepts' automated, pay-for-performance SEO technology platform called GravityStream; it fixes the inherent search engine unfriendliness of e-commerce platforms without the need for replatforming. GravityStream makes up the majority of our business today, although we also do plenty of consulting on SEO and online marketing.

We all understand the importance of optimizing a Web site to generate traffic, but how about optimizing a site for conversions? Why does this critical step seem to be an overlooked practice by most Web site owners?

SEO has been around a long time—since the 1990s. Conversion optimization as a practice hasn't been around as long and so hasn't had as much time to mature. But its day is coming—mark my words on that. As conversion optimization goes mainstream, another discipline is incubating and will develop into the next big thing.

What are the most common obstacles to conversion success you see on Web sites today?

In my experience it's software, software, software. Specifically it's the software that powers your Web site, such as your content management system or e-commerce platform. I also think it's a tough balancing act to maximize both SEO and conversion simultaneously. For example, stripping away much of the navigation from a landing page will minimize distractions and keep the user focused on completing the transaction. Yet we want to provide the search engine spiders with direct pathways into all of the important sections of the site, which would argue for leaving the navigation intact on the landing pages.

When you approached your last project, what did your plan for optimizing for conversions look like? What critical items had to be covered in the project?

The plan includes first the application of best practices and what I like to call advanced common sense. After that comes the multivariate testing or split tests, since human behavior is not always predictable. In addition, it's of immense value to conduct usability testing on a small group of people—like four to six. The usability testing does not have to be fancy, sophisticated, or expensive. A camcorder, tripod, clipboard, and room with a computer setup are about all you need. Oh, and $50 for each participant.

The following all have an impact on conversion: information architecture, layout, design, ontology, calls-to-action, value proposition/unique selling proposition, headline, page length, download speed, and more. Also don't neglect to analyze the search results listing. The components of the search listing—the title tag, meta description, and URL—all affect the click-through rate from the search results and, thus, indirectly, the conversion rate.

Based on your own experiences, which of the main channels have worked best in terms of generating traffic that converts?

For us at Netconcepts, it's been organic search. That said, the quality of the organic search traffic varies widely depending on many factors, such as the search engine, the query, and the stage in the buying cycle that the searcher's query represents. Google Images searchers convert poorly because they are looking to appropriate your images for their own use (like on their blog). A "long tail" search term that contains a model number or multiple product attributes signify that the searcher already did his or her homework and is probably ready to buy.

Please share with us three things readers can apply to their own Web sites today to help them increase conversions.

Add "social proof" to the landing page. This could take the form of testimonials. You can never have too many testimonials. But it doesn't have to be testimonials; it could be, for instance, the number of minutes/hours ago that each of the latest 10 customers bought from you, rendered anonymous, of course. Make sure it's "above the fold" too.

Not doing usability testing? What a shame! You're leaving money on the table. Conduct a usability test on-the-cheap by recruiting friends, family, acquaintances, and others. Use a camcorder and tripod.

Reinforce to search engine visitors that the landing page is about what they are looking for by dynamically inserting the their search term and/or crucial keywords from your paid search ad (sponsored listing) onto the landing page.

Any other words of wisdom to share with readers around increasing conversions?

If you haven't yet developed any personas for your Web site visitors, you really should sit down and start writing some. Then develop content specifically targeted to each of these major visitor types, with the intent of moving the user down a particular conversion path.

Some user behavior is completely nonintuitive and may vary greatly by site/market/industry. As such, best practices aren't always what they are cracked up to be. In other words, your mileage *will* vary. Conventional wisdom may be to use orange buttons because they convert better, but your users may respond better to blue buttons.

That wraps up our expert interviews. I sincerely hope they provided value and inspiration to you. The folks who lent their time, knowledge, and wisdom here are truly some of the best and brightest of today's online entrepreneurs. They have followed different paths to success and have learned many common lessons along the way. In the next and final chapter you will find some case studies that truly reveal the power of conversion optimization.

14

Case Studies

To wrap things up, in this chapter you will find some case studies that illuminate the effect of optimizing your conversion process. Karl Blanks and Ben Jesson at Conversion Rate Experts, whom you met in the last chapter, get credit for pulling together this information. As you will see, there is a clear trend demonstrated in these studies: invest in optimization, and conversions increase. You can use these case studies as references when pitching for work to be performed on your company's Web site. So let's take a look at the dramatic effect you can have on increasing conversions if you spend the time optimizing the process. In short, these are success stories of turning clicks into customers!

Success Story: Def-Shop

Def-Shop.com provides Europe's largest selection of hip-hop clothing. Most of its sales are to the German market.

In April 2009, Def-Shop began working with Conversion Rate Experts to help increase Def-Shop's profits. Here are some of the areas in which the two companies collaborated:

- E-commerce sites have several core functions, one of which is "matchmaking"—the site needs to show products that the visitor is most likely to be interested in. There are several ways of doing this, such as product recommendation engines, search boxes, information architecture, and navigation. An analysis of Def-Shop's site revealed great opportunities for improving the information architecture and navigation.

- It's important to give visitors reasons to buy from your site rather than from your competitors' sites. Conversations with Def-Shop's staff revealed 10 compelling advantages to ordering from Def-Shop; for example, Def-Shop has the largest selection of merchandise, a great returns policy, and great credibility in the form of associations with MTV and hip-hop celebrities. This information was made prominent at key points in the conversion funnel.

- Many successful businesses are based around a community of customers who share the same passions, values, and interests. Def-Shop's CEO, Alexander Buchler, is passionate about hip-hop culture and feels that hip-hop lacks a cultural focus in Europe. Conversion Rate Experts has encouraged Alex to invest in creating a whole community around Def-Shop in order to make the company a focus for hip-hop culture rather than just a Web store. The first Def-Shop celebrity party was held in Berlin in August 2009. Community events such as this one will provide additional proof that investing in creating the community has value and focus users on their online marketing campaigns.

Results

Early tests on key pages have resulted in increases in conversion rates of 20 63, and 115 percent.

■ ■ ■ Success Story: Voices.com

Voices.com describes itself as being "the USA's number one marketplace for voice-over talent." Its Web site allows companies to easily find voice-over artists.

In early 2009, Voices.com began working with Conversion Rate Experts to increase Voice.com's conversion rate. Here are some of the things the company worked on:

- Adding proof to the home page had a huge effect: Voices.com had some impressive claims to fame—things that would influence prospective customers—that weren't clearly communicated on the Web site. For example, it transpired that Voices.com's customers included many large brand names.
- The site had two distinct types of visitor: voice-over artists and companies looking for voice-over artists. There was a great benefit from immediately and clearly segmenting these two types into separate conversion funnels.
- Often, the biggest obstacle facing prospects is that they don't understand what they are about to sign up for. Voices.com overcame this obstacle by adding clearly communicated demonstration videos.
- Sometimes when working within a company, it is easy to become blind to how outsiders see the company. Some of Conversion Rate Experts' wins came from taking material that was already created and moving it to more prominent parts of the sales funnel.

David Ciccarelli, the CEO of Voices.com, described the process as being a "fascinating and profitable experience."

Results

Within weeks conversion rates had increased by over 400 percent—from less than 5 to 22 percent.

Success Story: Sunshine.co.uk

Sunshine.co.uk is a UK-based travel agency offering low-cost holidays.
Here are some of the areas that we looked into:

- Looking at Sunshine's Web pages, it wasn't immediately clear why prospects should use Sunshine rather than a competitor. Sunshine surveyed its existing customers to understand why they preferred Sunshine. The resulting feedback was overwhelmingly positive, allowing Sunshine to compile a short list of key messages that needed to be communicated to prospects. The company created new Web pages, which provided an immediate increase in business.
- Sometimes Sunshine's prices were so cheap they were unbelievable. By clarifying the pricing, and what it included, the conversion rate increased by 19 percent.

Commenting on the £8 million improvement, Sunshine's coowner Chris Clarkson remarked, "Conversion rate optimization is the best investment we've ever made."

Results

Within weeks of beginning to work with Conversion Rate Experts, Sunshine experienced some impressive improvements: a 24 percent increase, a 19 percent increase, and a 25 percent increase—all of which added £8 million per year (that's about $13 million) to the company's sales.

■ ■ ■ Success Story: SOS Worldwide

SOS Worldwide is a leading B2B broker of office space. The recession hit its industry hard—the demand for office space had fallen—and SOS contacted Conversion Rate Experts to help it convert the large volume of traffic it received.

Here are some of the areas of work SOS found success with:

- Credibility is important on the Web; prospects seek reassurance that they're dealing with a trustworthy, authoritative company. During discussions, it transpired that SOS had been in business for longer than any of its competitors—SOS was the first business of its type—and it was used by some of the world's largest organizations. This information was added to the site's header.

- Conversion Rate Experts conducted extensive usability tests on the existing site and on competitors' sites. These revealed several issues—some of them subtle—that were stopping prospects from making contact with SOS.

- Conversations with the company's sales staff revealed that incoming phone calls were worth about 10 times as much as leads submitted via the company's lead generation Web page. Additional "phone us now" calls to action were added to the lead generation page to encourage prospects to call in.

- SOS was able to help clients negotiate better rates on their rents. In fact, such negotiation is one of the main advantages of using a broker. This information was made prominent—in fact, it was added to the headline.

- During conversations with clients, Conversion Rate Experts learned that there were many pitfalls associated with renting office space. SOS Worldwide acts on the behalf of clients, helping them avoid these traps. SOS did not communicate this aspect of service on its Web site, so it added a new section called "Seven Things No One Should Miss When Renting Office Space in 2009," which was also available as a downloadable report, in exchange for prospects' e-mail addresses.

SOS's chief operating officer, Steven Boyne, commented, "The 66 percent increase in leads has had a large effect on our profit. In addition, the CRO process has given us a deeper understanding of what makes our customers tick. Our staff enjoy the fact they're working at the forefront of technology, which is making it easier for us to attract new talent."

Results

After several weeks' of work with Conversion Rate Experts, SOS uploaded a new version of one of its Web pages, which increased leads by 66 percent.

■ ▧ ■ Success Story: SEOmoz

SEOmoz is one of the world's largest paid membership sites for Web marketing. In November 2008, SEOmoz started working with Conversion Rate Experts to apply conversion rate optimization (CRO) to its Web site.

The graph in Figure 14.1 shows the impact that CRO had on SEOmoz's business:

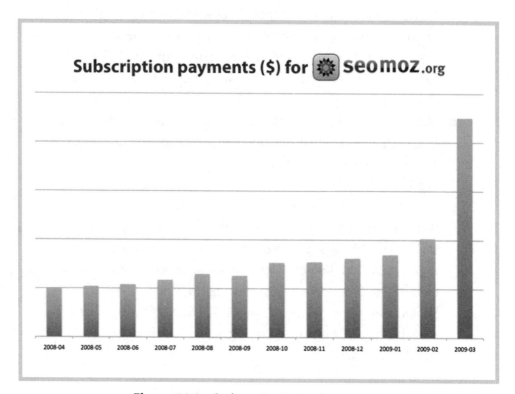

Figure 14.1. Subscription payments

SEOmoz's sales increased dramatically as a result of the tested improvements it implemented.

One of the things that contributed toward sales increase was a redesign of the landing page (Figure 14.2) for SEOmoz's paid subscription service.

Here are some of the items that were most fruitful in redesigning the landing page:

Figure 14.2. Landing page

In a phone call with Conversion Rate Experts, SEOmoz's CEO, Rand Fishkin, made a passing comment that whenever he was face-to-face with prospects, he was able to persuade them to subscribe to SEOmoz's paid service—but that the Web site was woefully inferior at persuading prospects to take action.

Conversion Rate Experts asked Rand to record the words that he used when he was selling face-to-face. The resulting nine-minute-long recorded sales message was then transcribed. It turned out that most of the information in it was not present in the existing landing page. The transcription was used to create the structure of the new page.

The new landing page was much longer than the original one; in fact, it was eight times as long. Many marketers have an aversion to creating long pages, but they can be extremely effective. (Just notice how long some of Amazon's pages are.) As a rule of thumb, you need at least as many words to sell something online as you need to sell it in person.

Because Rand was so effective at delivering the sales message in person, Conversion Rate Experts asked him to create a video of his sales message. The resulting video was embedded at the top of the landing page.

As can be seen in Figure 14.2, the headline of the new page was: "When eBay, Disney and Marriott need SEO help, here's what they do . . . " Headlines are incredibly important because they determine whether visitors will continue to read down the page. The first half of the new headline capitalized on the fact that, unlike some of its competitors, SEOmoz has a user base of sophisticated companies that are household names. This demonstrates credibility and provides evidence that SEOmoz's services are valuable. The second half of the headline (" . . . here's what they do . . . ") adds intrigue and indicates that readers will gain value from reading the page.

The page contains what offline direct marketers would call a "Johnson box"—effectively, a table of contents (in this case with hyperlinks to the corresponding content).

Perhaps surprisingly, many sales pages lack clear descriptions of what customers get. However, just such a detailed table was included in the new SEOmoz page, describing very clearly what users could expect to receive with their purchases.

A large number of testimonials were gathered from high-profile customers and added to the page (Figure 14.3).

Rand Fishkin said, "It has been remarkable to see the process in action, and to realize that this really is a process. Just like SEO, there's an art and a science to it."

These case studies are designed to show, at a top level, some success stories of businesses that took the time to optimize their conversion processes. Obviously, your results may vary, but these stories clearly indicate that by doing some work on your own Web site, you can potentially see big increases in conversions. All of the businesses referenced here agree on one point, though the approaches were different across the sites: time put into optimizing your conversion process is a wise investment.

Figure 14.3. Testimonials added to Web page

■ ■ ■ Conclusion

Thank you for reading through my book. I hope it has provided value for you in your journey to help turn clicks into conversions.

It doesn't matter whether you pursue search marketing and e-mail marketing, whether you produce Webinars or simply seek to drive traffic and monetize a Web site with advertising—there are a number of ways to generate revenue from almost any type of Web site. The lessons and information shared throughout this book should give you a good understanding of what it takes to begin generating traffic and increasing the revenue from your current traffic base. Each discipline mentioned could be a book unto itself. While Internet marketing may be relatively new, the adaptive learning we experienced over just the last decade on each of these topics has been impressive. You should embrace the idea of experimentation and explore multiple ways of increasing your conversions at the same time.

Finally, I wish you luck with your own online Web sites and projects. The Internet is almost limitless, and we have yet to realize its full commercial potential. As more people join the conversation and search for information online each year, the opportunities for Web entrepreneurs to carve out a successful niche continue to expand. I know you will be successful in your quest to generate more traffic and increase conversions simply because I once started fresh—with no understanding of Internet marketing—and today I run Web sites that successfully convert and develop revenue each month. The bottom line is that if I can do it, so can you!

Appendix 1

Name	URL	Language
Arab Tube	www.arabtube.tv	Arabic
Ikbis	ikbis.com	Arabic
56	www.56.com	Chinese
6.cn	6.cn	Chinese
Aeeboo	www.aeeboo.com	Chinese
KU6	www.ku6.com	Chinese
Mantou TV	www.mantoutv.com	Chinese
Mofile	tv.mofile.com	Chinese
Tudou	www.tudou.com	Chinese
Uume	uume.com	Chinese
Video.daqi	www.daqi.com	Chinese
Video.qq	video.qq.com	Chinese
You.video.sina.cn	v.sina.com.cn	Chinese
Youku	www.youku.com	Chinese
YouMaker	youmaker.com/video	Chinese
12 Seconds TV	12seconds.tv	English
4Shared	www.4shared.com	English
5min	www.5min.com	English
Aajkatv	www.aajkatv.com	English
Activist Video	www.activistvideo.org	English
AniBoom	www.aniboom.com	English

Name	URL	Language
ApnaTube	www.apnatube.com	English
Athena Web	www.athenaweb.org	English
Atom Films	www.atom.com	English
Babel Gum	www.babelgum.com	English
BGVIP TV	www.bgvip.tv	English
Big Contact	www.bigcontact.com	English
Big Think	www.bigthink.com	English
Blip TV	blip.tv	English
Blog Cheese	www.blogcheese.com	English
Blog TV	www.blogtv.com	English
BoFunk	www.bofunk.com	English
Bragster	www.bragster.com	English
Break	www.break.com	English
Broadband Sports	broadbandsports.com	English
Broadcaster	www.broadcaster.com	English
Buzz Net	www.buzznet.com	English
Cast Post	www.castpost.com	English
Caught On Video	www.caught-on-video.com	English
Clesh	clesh.com	English
Clevver	www.clevver.com	English
Clip Junkie	www.clipjunkie.com	English
Clip Moon	www.clipmoon.com	English
Clipser	www.clipser.com	English
Clone Videos	www.clonevideos.com	English
Cnet TV	cnettv.cnet.com	English
College Humor	www.collegehumor.com	English
Constant Comedy	constantcomedy.com	English
Cozmo TV	www.cozmo.tv	English
Crackle	www.crackle.com	English
Crunchy Roll	www.crunchyroll.com	English
Current TV	www.current.com/	English
Cuts	www.cuts.com	English
Da Nerd	www.danerd.com	English
Dada	us.dada.net/video	English
Daily Comedy	www.dailycomedy.com	English
Daily Motion	www.dailymotion.com	English

Name	URL	Language
Dalealplay	www.dalealplay.com	English
Dave TV	www.dave.tv	English
Dekhona	www.dekhona.com	English
Disclose TV	www.disclose.tv	English
Dogster	www.dogster.com/video	English
Dorks	www.dorks.com	English
Dot Comedy	www.dotcomedy.com	English
Dovetail TV	www.dovetail.tv	English
Drop Shots	www.dropshots.com	English
Drunkest	www.thedrunkest.com	English
Dump a Link	www.dumpalink.com	English
Dumpthe.net	www.dumpthe.net	English
E Snips	www.esnips.com	English
Ebaums World	www.ebaumsworld.com	English
Encyclomedia	www.encyclomedia.com	English
Engage Media	www.engagemedia.org	English
Entertaine	www.entertane.com	English
Everyzing	www.everyzing.com	English
Expo TV	www.expotv.com	English
Exprezzo	www.ezprezzo.com	English
Eye Spot	www.eyespot.com	English
Face Knock	www.faceknock.com	English
FameCast	www.famecast.com	English
Famster	www.famster.com	English
Fark	www.fark.com/video	English
File Cow	www.filecow.com	English
Fire Ant TV	www.fireant.tv	English
Flick Life	www.flicklife.com	English
Flickr	www.flickr.com	English
Flightlevel250	www.flightlevel350.com	English
Fliqz	www.fliqz.com	English
Flukiest	www.flukiest.com	English
Flurl	www.flurl.com	English
Free IQ	www.freeiq.com	English
Free V Log	www.freevlog.org	English
Fun Mansion	www.funmansion.com	English

Name	URL	Language
Funny Hub	www.funnyhub.com	English
Funny Junk	www.funnyjunk.com	English
Funny or Die	www.funnyordie.com	English
Funny Place	www.funnyplace.org	English
Funny Reign	www.funnyreign.com	English
GameTrailers	www.gametrailers.com	English
Get Miro	www.getmiro.com	English
Glumbert	www.glumbert.com	English
GodTube	www.godtube.com	English
Gorilla Mask	www.gorillamask.net	English
Graspr	www.graspr.com	English
Grind TV	www.grindtv.com	English
Grouper	www.grouper.com	English
Guzer	www.guzer.com	English
Heavy	www.Heavy.com	English
Helpful Video	www.helpfulvideo.com	English
Hictu	www.hictu.com	English
Holy Lemon	www.holylemon.com	English
Hook TV	www.hook.tv	English
HotShare Net	www.hotshare.net/en/share/videos	English
How Cast	www.howcast.com	English
Hulu	www.hulu.com	English
Hungry Flix	www.hungryflix.com	English
I Am Bored	www.i-am-bored.com	English
ICYou	icyou.com	English
Imeem	www.imeem.com	English
India Video	www.indiavideo.org	English
Internet Archive	www.archive.org/details/movies	English
Islamic Tube	www.islamictube.net	English
Jaycut	jaycut.com	English
Jokeroo	http://www.jokeroo.com	English
Joost	www.joost.com	English
Juju Nation	www.jujunation.com	English
Jumpcut	www.jumpcut.com	English
Just Video	www.justvideo.ca	English
Justin TV	www.justin.tv	English

Name	URL	Language
Kaneva	www.kaneva.com	English
Kewego	www.kewego.com	English
Kidzbop	www.kidzbop.com	English
KoldCast TV	www.koldcast.tv	English
Kyte TV	www.kyte.tv	English
Live Leak	www.liveleak.com	English
Live Video	www.livevideo.com	English
Lycos	mix.lycos.com	English
Magnify.net	www.magnify.net	English
Mania TV	www.maniatv.com	English
Matrix Movies	www.matrixmovies.net	English
Media Bum	www.mediabum.com	English
Metacafe	www.metacafe.com	English
Mind Bites	www.mindbites.com	English
Mob	www.mob.com	English
Mogulus	www.mogulus.com	English
Mojiti	mojiti.com	English
Mojo Flix	www.mojoflix.com	English
Monkee See	www.monkeysee.com	English
Motion Box	www.motionbox.com	English
Motor Sports Mad	www.motorsportmad.com	English
Multiply	multiply.com	English
Muslim Video	tv.muslimvideo.com	English
My Top Clip	www.mytopclip.com	English
My Video	www.myvideo.co.za	English
My Video Karaoke	www.myvideokaraoke.com	English
Mypraize	www.mypraize.com	English
MySpace TV	vids.myspace.com	English
MyToons	www.mytoons.com	English
Need for Fun	www.needforfun.com	English
Nelsok	www.nelsok.com	English
Ning	www.ning.com	English
On Fuego	www.onfuego.com	English
One True Media	www.onetruemedia.com	English
One World TV	tv.oneworld.net	English
ooVoo	www.oovoo.com	English

Name	URL	Language
Open Film	www.openfilm.com	English
Our Media	www.ourmedia.org	English
Ovi	share.ovi.com	English
Pandora TV	www.pandora.tv	English
Pawky	www.pawky.com	English
Photobucket	photobucket.com/recent/videos	English
Pickle	www.pickle.com	English
Pokertube	www.pokertube.com	English
Post Video Art	www.post-videoart.com	English
Pure Video	www.purevideo.com	English
Put File	www.putfile.com	English
Qube TV	www.qubetv.tv	English
Rambler Vision	vision.rambler.ru	English
Rediff	is.rediff.com	English
Revver	www.revver.com	English
Revver	revver.com	English
Rofl.to	www.rofl.to	English
Rooftop Comedy	www.rooftopcomedy.com	English
Scivee TV	www.scivee.tv	English
Sclipo	sclipo.com	English
Self Cast TV	www.selfcasttv.com	English
Sevenload	www.sevenload.com	English
Shout File	www.shoutfile.com	English
Show Me How to Play	www.showmehowtoplay.com	English
Show Medo	www.showmedo.com	English
Shred or Die	www.shredordie.com	English
Skill Tip TV	www.skilltip.tv	English
Snotr	www.snotr.com	English
Spike	www.spike.com/	English
Spiked Humor	www.spikedhumor.com	English
Spy Mac	www.spymac.com	English
Stage 6	stage6.divx.com	English
Street Fire	www.streetfire.net	English
Stupid Videos	www.stupidvideos.com	English
Sumo TV	www.sumo.tv	English
Tag World	www.tagworld.com	English

Name	URL	Language
Teacher Tube	www.teachertube.com	English
The Big TV	www.thebig.tv	English
The X Vid	www.thexvid.com	English
TinyPic	www.tinypic.com	English
Treemo	www.treemo.com	English
Troop Tube	www.trooptube.tv	English
Truveo	www.truveo.com	English
Tu TV	www.tu.tv	English
Tube Desi	www.tubedesi.com	English
Tubetorial	www.tubetorial.com	English
Tuney Fish	www.tuneyfish.com	English
Tvosz	www.tvosz.com	English
U2 Up Fly	www.u2upfly.com	English
Ustream	www.ustream.tv	English
Uvu.channel2.org	uvu.channel2.org	English
V Log Map	www.vlogmap.org	English
Vbox 7	vbox7.com	English
Veoh	www.veoh.com	English
Viddler	www.viddler.com	English
Viddyou	www.viddyou.com	English
Video Bomb	www.videobomb.com	English
Video Dumper	www.videodumper.com	English
Video Jug	videojug.com	English
Video Tabs	video-tabs.com	English
Video Vat	www.videovat.com	English
Video Web Town	www.videowebtown.com	English
Video123	www.video123.com	English
Videoontherocks. indya.com	videoontherocks.indya.com	English
Videos.streetfile.net	videos.streetfire.net	English
Vidiac	www.vidiac.com	English
Vidilife	www.vidilife.com	English
Vidipedia	www.vidipedia.org	English
Vidivodo	www.vidivodo.com	English
Vidmax	www.vidmax.com	English
Viewdo	www.viewdo.com	English

Name	URL	Language
Vimeo	www.vimeo.com	English
Vmix	www.vmix.com	English
Vod Pod	vodpod.com	English
Voomed	www.voomed.com	English
Vsocial	www.vsocial.com	English
Vuze	www.vuze.com	English
We Game	www.wegame.com	English
WebCastr	www.webcastr.com	English
WebShots	www.webshots.com	English
Wildscreen TV	www.wildscreen.tv	English
WonderHowTo	www.wonderhowto.com	English
WTF Humor	www.wtfhumor.com	English
Yahoo Video	video.yahoo.com	English
Yideoz	www.yideoz.com	English
Yikers	www.yikers.com	English
You Are TV	www.youare.tv	English
You3B	http://www.you3b.com	English
Your Daily Media	www.yourdailymedia.com	English
Your File Host	www.yourfilehost.com	English
YouTomb	youtomb.mit.edu	English
Youtube	www.youtube.com	English
Zapiks	www.zapiks.com/_videos_/	English
Zeec	www.zeec.net	English
Ziddo	www.ziddio.com	English
Zooppa	www.zooppa.com	English
Zoopy	www.zoopy.com/video/4	English
Daily Haha	www.dailyhaha.com	French
Eyeka	fr.eyeka.com	French
Video Click	www.videoclick.com	French
Wat.tv	www.wat.tv	French
Wideo.fr	www.wideo.fr	French
Autsch.de	autsch.de	German
Businessworld.de	businessworld.de	German
Citytube	citytube.de	German
Clip Fish	www.clipfish.de	German
Clip Host 24	www.cliphost24.com	German

Name	URL	Language
Cooxt.de	www.cooxt.de	German
Crovideos	www.crovideos.com	German
Deaf Video	www.deaf-video.org	German
Deutschlandreporter.de	www.deutschlandreporter.de	German
Evisor TV	www.evisor.tv/tv	German
Film Upload	www.filmupload.de	German
Fixx.tvspielfilm.de	fixx.tvspielfilm.de/videos	German
Getttyload.de	www.gettyload.de	German
Hamburg1video.de	www.hamburg1video.de	German
Hausgemacht.tv	hausgemacht.tv	German
Ikiwi.at	www.ikiwi.at	German
Kino.tv	www.kino.to	German
Learn 2 Use	www.learn2use.de	German
Live.focus.de	live.focus.de/videos	German
Living Zurich TV	livingzurich.tv	German
Lost-on-stage.de	www.lost-on-stage.de	German
Luegmol.ch	www.luegmol.ch	German
Lustich.de	lustich.de/videos	German
Myspass.de	www.myspass.de	German
MyVideo.de	www.myvideo.de	German
Petnet.de	www.petnet.de	German
Rhin Video	www.rheinvideo.de	German
Spotn.de	www.spotn.de	German
Talentrun.de	www.talentrun.de	German
TV1.at	www.tv1.at	German
TVBVideo.de	www.tvbvideo.de	German
Uprom TV	www.uprom.tv	German
Video Community	www.videocommunity.com	German
Video.vol.at	video.vol.at	German
Video.web.de	video.web.de	German
Video.youteach.de	video.youteach.de	German
Zap Live	www.zaplive.tv	German
Zeec.de	zeec.de	German
Libero	video.libero.it	Italian
EyeVio.jp	eyevio.jp	Japanese
Flip Clip	www.flipclip.net	Japanese

Name	URL	Language
Vision.Ameba.jp	vision.ameba.jp	Japanese
Vidoosh TV	www.vidoosh.tv	Persian
RuTube	rutube.ru	Russian
Smotri	smotri.com	Russian
Upload-fest.ru	www.upload-fest.ru	Russian
Myubo.sk	www.myubo.sk	Slovak
Bubblare	www.bubblare.se	Swedish
Fejmtv.se	www.fejmtv.se	Swedish
Miloop.se	www.miloop.se	Swedish
Video Klipp	www.video-klipp.se	Swedish
Duclip	www.duclip.com	Thai
Video.eksenim.mynet	video.eksenim.mynet.com	Turkish
Clip.vn	clip.vn	Vietnamese

Appendix 2

Name	Description/Focus	Registration
Adult FriendFinder	Adults only dating/hook-up network	Open
Advogato	Free and open source software developers	Open
Amie Street	Music	Open
ANobii	Books	Open
aSmallWorld	European jet set and social elite	Invite-only
Athlinks	Running, swimming	Open
Avatars United	Online games	Open
Badoo	General; popular in Europe	Open to people 18 and older
Bebo	General	Open to people 13 and older
Bigadda	Indian social networking site	Open to people 16 and older
Biip	Norwegian community	Requires Norwegian phone number
BlackPlanet	African Americans	Open
Broadcaster.com	Video sharing and Webcam chat	Open
Buzznet	Music and pop culture	Open
CafeMom	Mothers	Open to moms and moms-to-be
Cake Financial	Investing	Open
Care2	Green living and social activism	Open

Name	Description/Focus	Registration
Classmates.com	School, college, work, and the military	Open
Cloob	General; popular in Iran	Open
College Tonight	College students	Requires an e-mail address with an .edu ending
CouchSurfing	Worldwide network for making connections between travelers and the local communities they visit	Open
DailyStrength	Medical and emotional support community; physical health, mental health, support groups	Open
DeviantART	Art community	Open
Disaboom	People with disabilities; amputee, cerebral palsy, MS, and other disabilities	Open
dol2day	Politics community, social network, Internet radio (German-speaking countries)	Open
DontStayIn	Clubbing (primarily UK)	Open
Draugiem.lv	General (primarily LV, LT, HU)	Invite-only
Elftown	Community and wiki around fantasy and sci-fi	Open; approval needed
Epernicus	Research scientists	Open
Eons.com	Baby boomers	Open to people 13 and older
Experience Project	Life experiences	Open
Exploroo	Travel and social networking	Open
Facebook	General	Open to people 13 and older
Faceparty	General; popular in UK	Invite-only to people 18 and older
Faces.com	British teens	Open to people 13 and older
Fetlife	People who are into BDSM	Open to people "of (legal) age to see adult content"
Filmaffinity	Movies and TV series	Open
FledgeWing	Entrepreneurial community targeted toward worldwide university students	Open to university students

Name	Description/Focus	Registration
Flixster	Movies	Open to people 13 and older
Flickr	Photo sharing, commenting, photography related networking; worldwide	Open to people 13 and older
Fotolog	Photoblogging; popular in South America and Spain	Open
Friends Reunited	UK based; school, college, work, sport, and streets	Open to people 13 and older
Friendster	General; popular in Southeast Asia; no longer popular in the Western world	Open to people 16 and older; no children allowed
Frühstückstreff	General	Open
Fubar	Dating; an "online bar" for 18 and older	Open
Gaia Online	Anime and games	Open to people 13 and older
GamerDNA	Computer and video games	Open
Gather.com	Article, picture, and video sharing, as well as group discussions	Open
Geni.com	Families, genealogy	Open
Gogoyoko	Fair play in music; social networking site for musicians and music lovers	Invite-only while in beta
Goodreads	Library cataloging, book lovers	Open
Gossipreport.com	Anonymous gossip	Open to people 16 and older
Grono.net	Poland	Open
Habbo	General for teens; over 31 communities worldwide; chat room and user profiles	Open to people 13 and older
hi5	General; popular in India, Portugal, Mongolia, Thailand, Romania, Jamaica, Central Africa, and Latin America; not popular in the United States	Open to people 13 and older; no children allowed
Hospitality Club	Hospitality	Open
Hyves	General; most popular in the Netherlands	Open

Name	Description/Focus	Registration
ibibo	Talent-based social networking site that allows promotion of oneself and also discovers new talent; most popular in India	Open
imeem	Music, video, photos, blogs	Open
IRC-Galleria	Finland	Open to Finnish-speaking people 12 and older
italki.com	Language-learning social network; 100+ languages	Open; global
InterNations	International community	Invite-only
itsmy	Mobile community worldwide; blogging, friends, personal TV shows	Invite-only
iWiW	Hungary	
Jaiku	General; owned by Google	Open to people 13 and older
Jammer Direct	Creative resource Web site	Open to the general public
kaioo	General; nonprofit	
Kaixin001	General; in simplified Chinese; caters for mainland China users	Open to the general public
Kiwibox	General; for the users and by the users; a social network that is more than a community;	Open to people 13 and older
Last.fm	Music	Open to people 13 and older
LibraryThing	Book lovers	Open to people 13 and older
lifeknot	Shared interests, hobbies	Open to people 18 and older
LinkedIn	General but mainly business	Open to people 18 and older
LiveJournal	Blogging	Open (OpenID)
Livemocha	Online language learning; dynamic online courses in 22 languages; world's largest community of native language speakers	Open
LunarStorm	Sweden	Open
MEETin	General	Open
Meetup.com	General; used to plan offline meetings for people interested in various activities	Open to people 18 and older

Name	Description/Focus	Registration
Meettheboss	Business and finance community; worldwide	Open
Mixi	Japan	Invite-only
mobikade	Mobile community; UK only	Open to people 18 and older
MocoSpace	Mobile community; worldwide	Open to people 14 and older
MOG	Music	Open to people 14 and older
Multiply	"Real world" relationships; popular in Asia; not popular in the Western world	Open to people 13 and older; no children allowed
Muxlim	Muslim portal site	Open to people 13 and older
MyAnimeList	Anime themed social community	Open to people 13 and older
MyChurch	Christian churches	Open
MyHeritage	Family-oriented social network service	Open
MyLife	Locating friends and family, keeping in touch (formerly Reunion.com)	Open
MyLOL	General; popular in the United States, Europe, and Australia	Open to people 13 and older
MySpace	General	Open to people 13 and older
myYearbook	General	Open to people 13 and older and grades 9 and up
Nasza-klasa.pl	School, college, and friends; popular in Poland	Open
Netlog	General; popular in Europe and Québec province; formerly known as Facebox and Redbox	Open to people 13 and older
Nettby	Norwegian community	Open
Nexopia	Canada	Open to people 14 and older
Ning	Users create their own social Web sites and social networks	Open to people 13 and older
Odnoklassniki	General; popular in Russia and former Soviet republics	Open
OkCupid	Social networking and dating	Open to people 18 and older
OneClimate	Not-for-profit social networking and climate change	Open to people of all ages and locations

Name	Description/Focus	Registration
OneWorldTV	Not-for-profit video sharing and social networking aimed at people interested in social issues, development, environment, etc.	Open
Open Diary	First online blogging community; founded in 1998	Open to people 13 and older
Orkut	Owned by Google; popular in Brazil	Open to people 18 and older (Google log-in)
OUTeverywhere	Gay/LGBTQ community	Open
Passportstamp	Travel	Open
Pingsta	Collaborative platform for the world's Internetwork experts	Invite-only; only Internet experts
Plaxo	Aggregator	Open
Playahead	Swedish, Danish, Norwegian teenagers	Open
Playboy U	Online college community	Open to college students with .edu e-mail address
Plurk	Microblogging, RSS, updates	Open
Present.ly	Enterprise social networking and microblogging	Open
Qapacity	A business-oriented social networking site and a business directory	Open to people 16 and older
quarterlife	A social network for artists, filmmakers, musicians, and other creative people	Open to people 14 and older
Ravelry	Knitting and crocheting	Invite-only while in beta
ResearchGATE	Social network for scientific researchers	Open
Reverbnation	Social network for musician and bands	Open to people 16 and older
Ryze	Business	Open
scispace.net	Collaborative network site for scientists	By invitation, but can request an invitation
Shelfari	Books	Open
Skyrock	Social network in French-speaking world	Open

Name	Description/Focus	Registration
SocialGO	A social network builder that allows users to build their own online communities	Open to people 18 and older
SocialVibe	Social network for charity	Open
Sonico.com	General; popular in Latin America and Spanish- and Portuguese-speaking regions	Open to people 13 and older
Soundpedia	Music	Open
Stickam	Live video streaming and chat	Open
StudiVZ	University students, mostly in German-speaking countries; school students and those out of education sign up via its partner sites SchulerVZ and Meinvz	Open
Supernova.com	Link to people who share the same passion for indie music; connect with indie bands, music fans, and the indie music scene; Supernova.com is the only online music community that actively promotes its bands by producing Battle of the Bands live shows to showcase music and talents; sign up on Supernova.com to find gigs, play live shows, discover new bands, and listen to new indie music	Open
Tagged.com	General	Open
Talkbiznow	Business networking	Open
Taltopia	Online artistic community	Open
TravBuddy.com	Travel	Open to people 18 and older
Travellerspoint	Travel	Open
tribe.net	General	Open
Trombi.com	French subsidary of Classmates.com	Open

Name	Description/Focus	Registration
Tuenti.com	Spanish-based university and high school social network; very popular in Spain	Invite-only
Tumblr	General; microblogging, RSS	Open
Twitter	General; microblogging, RSS, updates	Open
V Kontakte	Russian social network	Open
Vampirefreaks	Gothic and industrial subculture	Open to users 13 and over
Viadeo	European social networking and campus networking in seven languages	Open
Vox	Blogging	Open
Wakoopa	For computer fans who want to discover new software and games	Open
Wasabi	General	Open
WAYN	Travel and lifestyle	Open to people 18 and older
WebBiographies	Genealogy and biography	Open
Windows Live Spaces	Blogging (formerly MSN Spaces)	Open
WiserEarth	Online community space for the social justice and environmental movement	Open to people 18 and older
Xanga	Blogs and "metro" areas	Open
Xiaonei	Significant site in China	Open
XING	Business, primarily Europe (Germany, Austria, Switzerland) and China	Open
Xt3	Catholic social networking, created after World Youth Day 2008	Open
Yammer	Social networking for office colleagues	Must have company e-mail
Yelp, Inc.	Local business review and talk	Open
Youmeo	UK social network (focus on data portability)	Open
Zoo.gr	Greek Web meeting point	Open

Index

About the Author

DUANE FORRESTER is a senior program manager with Microsoft, running its internal SEO program for MSN. He's also the founding co-chair of SEMPO's in-house SEM Committee, sits on the board of directors with SEMPO, and is the author of the successful book *How to Make Money with Your Blog*.

Duane finds time to help as a moderator at www.searchengineforums.com, and he maintains his own blog at www.theonlinemarketingguy.com. He writes a monthly column for www.searchengineland.com, where he discusses in-house search marketing, with an emphasis on its management and on prominent people in the industry today.

A few times a year, you can find Duane speaking at the main search marketing conferences held around the United States.

Otherwise, Duane enjoys walking his dogs and riding his motorcycle.